The
'Dictatorship of the Proletariat'
from
Marx to Lenin

The
'Dictatorship of the Proletariat'
from
Marx to Lenin

Hal Draper

MONTHLY REVIEW PRESS
New York

Library of Congress Cataloging-in-Publication Data
Draper, Hal.
    The "dictatorship of the proletariat" from Marx to Lenin.

    Bibliography: p.
    Includes index.
    1. Dictatorship of the proletariat.   2. Marx,
Karl, 1818–1883.   3. Lenin, Vladimir Il'ich, 1870–1924.   I. Title.
JC474.D734   1987   320.5'32
ISBN 0-85345-727-1
ISBN 0-85345-726-3 (pbk.)

Monthly Review Press
155 West 23rd Street
New York, N.Y. 10011

Manufactured in the United States of America

10 9 8 7 6 5 4 3 2 1

Contents

Preface

This book is a sequel, a continuation of the story told in my *Karl Marx's Theory of Revolution,* Volume 3, "The 'Dictatorship of the Proletariat.'" In *KMTR* 3, in accordance with the general plan of that work, I carried the account up through Marx and Engels themselves, that is, to 1895. But of course this was only the first chapter in the history of the phrase that later became so famous.

The phrase became world famous not because of its use by Marx or Engels but because of the role it played in the world revolutionary upsurge after the First World War and in the world Communist movement, particularly its use by the Russian Bolshevik government to describe its revolutionary state. It was put to two uses.

On the one hand, the word 'dictatorship' by itself had increasingly come to mean, since the latter part of the nineteenth century, something antidemocratic, the opposite of control by popular sovereignty. By this time the counterposition of the terms 'dictatorship' and 'democracy' had only recently become possible, though this counterposition was not yet as clear-cut as it later became. The term 'dictatorship' still trailed some of its previous history, which we will review in Chapter 1. Still, the relatively new denotation of 'dictatorship' was strong enough to provide the international anti-Soviet campaign with added material to depict the Russian Revolution as simply the imposition of a new despotism over the country. *(You see, they themselves admit that it's a dictatorship!)**

---

*I suggest the hypothesis that it was this worldwide campaign itself that permanently *fixed* the meaning of 'dictatorship' in the contemporary form, and put an end to the period when the old and new meanings were jostling and overlapping. Another opinion

7

On the other hand, the Bolsheviks, along with the world Communist movement they had sponsored, tied the phrase up with the revolutionary side of Marxism; for had not Marx devised it and used it as a designation for a truly revolutionary regime? So they believed.

In any case, as we will see, the phrase became a terminological football to be kicked about in the political war over a much more important question: the destiny and character of the Russian Revolution and the workers' Soviet government it had ushered into existence for the first time in the history of the world. On both sides few, if any, of the polemists were much concerned with what old Marx had been talking about when he first wrote the term down in 1850. Yet all pretended to be debating the meaning of Marx's revolutionary socialism or communism, and many of them sincerely believed that this was what they were about.

This was the pattern acted out in 1919–20, when Kautsky issued his brochure titled *The Dictatorship of the Proletariat* and Lenin replied bitterly with *The Proletarian Revolution and the Renegade Kautsky*. We will see that neither side in this controversy can be understood if we think, as did the participants, that it proceeded from the views of Marx and Engels.

Then, later in the 1920s, the term entered into its final phase: its transmogrification under Stalin into *nothing* but a code word for a totalitarian dictatorship over the people; its final evisceration of all revolutionary-democratic content. This last part of the story is relatively simple, and will not concern us; discussion of what was called the 'dictatorship of the proletariat' in this last period would be purely and simply a discussion of the nature and operation of the new bureaucratic-collectivist society established in Russia. The term was now only a bureaucratic watchword.

The question for the present book is this: what happened to the term 'dictatorship of the proletariat' between the death of Engels in 1895 and the definitive imposition of the Stalinist regime in the 1920s? The job is to cover two areas in particular: the history of the phrase in the Second International, and its history in the Russian movement from Plekhanov to Lenin.

---

has it that this final stage of the word was due to the emergence of the fascist dictatorships a little later. But even this view must admit that the international campaign against the "dictatorship of the proletariat" must have prepared the ground for, and then reinforced, the vocabulary developed to discuss fascism.

This is a difficult task because little or no serious historical work has been done on this aspect of the socialist movement by either academic or political writers. I am by no means satisfied that I have pulled together all of the historical threads; it is a question of an initial or ground-breaking contribution to the story.

At the risk of repeating the obvious, I must remind the reader that— as I wrote in the Foreword to *KMTR* 3—I am not dealing with the dictatorship of the proletariat but with the 'dictatorship of the proletariat,' that is, with the term or locution. It is a limited corner of a big subject. Its interest is that it throws some light on the big subject, perhaps only a sidelight, but its limited character must be kept in mind.

This is especially true in connection with the knotty and bitterly controversial problems revolving around the Russian Revolution. Here I am dealing with a single item in the history of political theory, somewhat arbitrarily separated off from the larger questions of the Revolution and Lenin's role in it. It should be plain that Lenin's tacking and veering on the subject of the *term* was intimately related to his changing political course vis-à-vis the revolution as a whole. Indeed, in one section (Chapter 4, Section 5, "The Steel Wire") I have tried to connect my subject up with the most important aspect of the political context; but this, I think, is as much as I can do without writing the millionth book about the problems of the Russian Revolution.

All this applied essentially also to the historical account in *KMTR* 3, on the development of the phrase by Marx, what it meant to him, and how he and Engels used it in their own writings. Chapter 1 is a summary of this material.* This chapter, unlike the rest of this book, gives its source references in terms of the volume it is summarizing; anyone who wants to look up the evidence for my summary statements will have to go to the detailed information in *KMTR*.

This book follows the practices of *KMTR* in a number of technical respects.

• *Notes.* There is a sharp distinction between *reference notes,* which are relegated to the back of the book, and *footnotes,* which are intended

---

*But there is a great deal of other material in *KMTR* 3 which is not included in Chapter 1, in particular on Blanqui and Blanquism and Marx's relation thereto. Nor does Chapter 1 cover a number of sections of related history in *KMTR*, such as the story of SUCR, Moses Hess and dictatorship, etc.

to be read as part of the text. General readers are advised to ignore all the superscript numbers that pepper the pages, unless of course they seek the source information to which the reference notes are devoted. The reference notes sometimes deal with other technical matters, but they never affect or contribute to the line of thought.

• *Quotes.* Inside quoted passages, all emphasis is in the original, and all [bracketed words] represent my own interpolations.

• *Translations.* All translations or revisions of translations not otherwise ascribed are my own responsibility.

• *Single quote marks.* In this book, single quotes are used to mark off words or phrases that are being used as *terms,* instead of italicizing them to show this usage, as is often done. Double quotes, as usual, denote words actually being quoted from a speaker or writer. The following examples show three different usages:

—The proletariat grew in numbers during the Industrial Revolution.

—'Proletariat' was first used in the Roman census of the sixth century B.C.

—Blanqui said he belonged to the "proletariat."

—*Falsifiction.* My Foreword to *KMTR* 3 explains that I occasionally use this word, as distinct from "falsification," to denote the statement of the false without any necessary intention to deceive. This practice continues in the present volume, in order to put the emphasis not on any claim of falsification but only on the differentiation of falsifiction from fact.

1

The 'Dictatorship
of the Proletariat'
in Marx and Engels

The phrase 'dictatorship of the proletariat' first appeared in a series of articles by Marx, later titled *The Class Struggles in France 1848–1850*, published in what was then Marx's own London magazine. The first article, written in January 1850, came off the press in early March. The expression or its equivalent appeared not once but three times—in each of the three installments (or chapters) that comprised the original series.

This work was Marx's attempt to sum up the political meaning of the European revolution of 1848–49. Marx had taken an active part in this revolution in the German arena, as editor of the leading organ on the revolutionary left, at the same time closely following the turbulent developments in France and Vienna in particular. The revolution was now over, and Marx was thinking over its lessons.

The first question is: when it appeared in print in the spring of 1850, what did the phrase mean to Marx and to his contemporaneous readers?

The key fact, which was going to bedevil the history of the term, is this: in the middle of the nineteenth century the old word 'dictatorship' still meant what it had meant for centuries, and in this meaning it was *not* a synonym for despotism, tyranny, absolutism, or autocracy, and above all it was *not* counterposed to democracy.

1. Short Sketch of 'Dictatorship'

The word 'dictatorship' in all languages (*dictature, Diktatur,* etc.) began as a reference to the *dictatura* of the ancient Roman Republic, an important constitutional institution that lasted for over three centuries and left its enduring mark on all political thought. This institution provided for an emergency exercise of power by a trusted citizen for temporary and limited purposes, for six months at the most. Its aim was to preserve the republican status quo; it was conceived to be a bulwark in defense of the republic against a foreign foe or internal subversion; indeed it was directed *against* elements whom we might today accuse of wanting "dictatorship." It worked—at least until Julius Caesar destroyed the republican *dictatura* by declaring himself un-limited "dictator" in permanence, that is, a dictator in our present-day sense.[1]

The modern analogue of the Roman *dictatura* is the institution of martial law (or "state of siege"). This device has the three distinguish-ing features of the Roman one: it is based on constitutional legality, not tyranny; it is temporary; it is limited, especially in its ability to impose new laws or constitutions. Again and again, institutions of the martial-law type have provided for some form of crisis government or emergency regime. Few claim that these institutions are *ipso facto* antidemocratic, though of course they can be perverted to anti-democratic uses like everything else.[2]

The old meaning conditioned all European political thought and language right into the nineteenth century, though the application of the term tended to blur in some respects. Most consistently it kept referring to an emergency management of power, especially outside of normal legality. The one-man aspect of its meaning was sometimes primary, but it was often muffled, particularly by rightists attacking the dominance of a popularly elected body.[3]

In the French Revolution—like all revolutions a bubbling cauldron of political terminology—the Girondins liked to denounce the "dic-tatorship of the National Convention" (the zenith of revolutionary democracy at the time) or the "dictatorship of the Commune of Paris" (the most democratic expression yet seen of a mass movement from below).[4] For over a century no one would blink when the British Parliament was attacked as a "dictatorship" on the ground that it held all power, though this usage dropped even the crisis-government aspect of the term.

The history of 'dictatorship' on the left begins with the very first socialist-communist movement, the first fusion of the socialistic idea with membership organization: the so-called "Conspiracy of the Equals" led by Babeuf in 1796, in the backwash of the failed French Revolution. In an influential book published in 1828, Babeuf's lieutenant Buonarroti described the activity and politics of this movement in some detail, thereby producing a textbook of Jacobin-communist politics that helped educate (and miseducate) the "Blanquist" leftists of the next two decades. (It was quickly published in English by left Chartists.)

Buonarroti described the conspirators' discussion on the transitional revolutionary government to take power after victory. While eschewing the term 'dictatorship' because of its one-man meaning, he left no doubt that the revolutionary government was to be the dictatorship of the small band making the revolution, which had the task of educating the people up to the level of eventual democracy. This concept of Educational Dictatorship was going to have a long future before it. There was not the slightest question of a 'dictatorship' *of*, or *by*, the workingpeople, corrupted as they were by the exploitive society to be overthrown. The revolutionary band of idealistic dictators alone would exercise the transitional dictatorship, for an unspecified period of time, at least a generation.[5]

This was also the entire content of the concept of dictatorship held by Auguste Blanqui and the Blanquist bands of the thirties and forties. In addition, the Blanquists (and not only they) advocated the "dictatorship of Paris" over the provinces and the country as a whole— which meant, above all, over the peasants and the rural artisanry; for had not the provinces shown in the Great Revolution that they tended toward counterrevolution? In the name of The People, the revolutionary saviors would defend the revolution against the people.

Incidentally, the ascription of the term 'dictatorship of the proletariat' to Blanqui is a myth industriously copied from book to book by marxologists eager to prove that Marx was a putschist "Blanquist"; but in fact all authorities on Blanqui's life and works have (sometimes regretfully) announced that the term is not to be found there. More important, the concept of political power exercised by the democratic masses is basically alien to the Blanquist idea of Educational Dictatorship.[6]

By the nineteenth century political language had long included references to the "dictatorship" of the most democratic assemblies, of popular mass movements, or even of The People in general. All Marx did at the time was apply this old political term to the political power of a *class*.

But Marx's usage in 1850 was significantly conditioned not merely by the long history of the word but particularly by its history in the revolutionary period he had just passed through.

2. 'Dictatorship' in the 1848 Revolution

Revolutions are by nature periods of crisis management and emergency power, in which the old legalities totter or tumble. This is true on both sides, for counterrevolutions are no greater respecters of legality. The revolution of 1848 saw the imposition of a "dictatorship," that of General Cavaignac, which was the herald of its modern history. But the necessity of some sort of dictatorship (in the terminology of the day) was recognized on all sides and freely discussed by the most disparate political tendencies from right to left.[7]

The essential meaning of 'dictatorship' at this time can be seen best in the case of Louis Blanc, one of the pinkest social-democrats in the early history of the movement. He constituted the left wing of the provisional government that took power in the February Revolution. This government naturally assumed power extralegally, through an announcement before a mass demonstration. Even Lamartine, its right-wing leader who was anxious to lead the revolution into conservative channels, called himself and his colleagues "dictators" for this reason. Louis Blanc *advocated* the continuance of the "dictatorship," through the postponement of elections, in order to allow for a period of re-education of the people. Not only at the time but in a book published ten years later, Blanc advocated that the provisional government should "regard themselves as dictators appointed by a revolution which had become inevitable and which was under no obligation to seek the sanction of universal suffrage until after having accomplished all the good which the moment required." Blanc not only wanted a longer postponement than did the revolutionary workers' clubs of Paris, he also advocated the old idea of the "dictatorship of Paris" over the country.[8]

Obviously 'dictatorship' was not the property of "extremists" and wild-eyed revolutionaries. Far from being counterposed to democracy, it was viewed—favorably or hostilely—as an aspect of the movement of the Democracy.

Everyone had his own idea of what the proper sort of 'dictatorship' should be. Wilhelm Weitling had long advocated a messianic dictatorship with himself as the messiah, and in 1848 he openly advocated a dictatorship with a "single head"; a couple of weeks later, Marx attacked and rejected Weitling's proposal in the same forum that Weitling had used.[9] Bakunin, involved in the revolutionary movement in Bohemia, later recounted that his aim was the establishment of a "government with unlimited dictatorial power," in which "all will be subjugated to a single dictatorial authority," through three secret societies based on "strict hierarchy and unconditional discipline." This was only the first version of Bakunin's lifelong fabrication of various forms of a "secret dictatorship" exercised by "Invisible Dictators."[10]

These concepts of 'dictatorship' (and others) were plainly anti-democratic, just as most concepts of 'government' were anti-democratic. But, like the word 'government,' 'dictatorship' could be filled with various contents, denoting some extralegal sort of emergency regime; and it was. In the "June days" of 1848, when the Paris working class erupted in the greatest revolt that modern history had yet seen, the panic-stricken provisional government replied by entrusting the power of military "dictatorship" to General Cavaignac, who used it for an educational bloodletting on a mass scale even after the fighting was over. (The term 'dictatorship' was not used officially, but was common in the press and on everyone's tongue; the official term was "state of siege.")

To be sure, Cavaignac's dictatorship was not a modern dictatorship, but it was the prelude to the modern history of the term. It provided the juridical basis for the state-of-siege provision put into the French constitution of November 1848, which in turn led to the law of August 9, 1849, still in force in the twentieth century as the basic law of "constitutional dictatorship" in France. It provided the model for martial-law institutions in Berlin and Vienna later in 1848. It cleared the way for the dictatorship of Napoleon III, which did not call itself a dictatorship but merely the Second Empire. It made dictatorship a European institution.[11]

During this revolution Marx was the dominant figure on the extreme left of the revolution in Germany, as editor of the *Neue*

Rheinische Zeitung in Cologne. Like everyone else, the *N.R.Z.* referred to dictatorship. But the first mention of 'dictatorship' in its columns was not by Marx but occurred in a quotation from the head of the provisional government that had taken power in the revolution behind the mass surge of revolt—and which was determined to prevent the revolution from overthrowing the Crown and its absolutist government. The prime minister, Camphausen, a Rhenish capitalist, strenuously argued that if the provisional government and its assembly took sovereign power in the name of the popular rule, this would be a "dictatorship"—the dictatorship of the Democracy indeed. If the new government democratized the elite system of voting, this would be dictatorship too.

Now the main line championed by Marx's *N.R.Z.* was the simple proposal that the National Assembly declare itself sovereign, repudiating the absolutist government and appealing to the people. No one doubted that this raised the question of revolutionary legality. That is what revolutions are for. The term 'dictatorship' on all sides simply reflected this problem, as Camphausen had exemplified by his attack on the dictatorship of the Democracy. It was in this context that the *N.R.Z.* advocated that the 'dictatorship' of the popular assembly put through a whole series of democratizing measures to revolutionize Germany's autocratic society. Marx wrote:

> Every provisional state setup after a revolution requires a dictatorship, and an energetic dictatorship at that. From the beginning we taxed Camphausen with not acting dictatorially, with not immediately smashing and eliminating the remnants of the old institutions.

There was no question of a 'dictatorship of the proletariat' here because Marx's policy in this revolution was to champion the initial assumption of power not by the working-class movement (which was just getting organized) but by the liberal bourgeoisie, whose historical task it was (as Marx then saw it) to uproot the old regime of Crown-bureaucracy-feudalists and establish a bourgeois democratic society, in which the proletariat could develop its own movement and its own class struggle looking toward eventual victory. But the German bourgeoisie, in large part precisely because it saw a revolutionary proletariat pressing behind it, refused to play out this drama, and instead clung to the absolutist government's power as its bulwark against the future proletarian threat.

The most important lesson that Marx learned from the revolutionary experience was that the German bourgeoisie could not be relied on to make its *own* revolution, the bourgeois democratic revolution which would eventually lay the basis for the proletarian socialist revolution. The two tasks would have to be telescoped, unlike the pattern that France had exemplified. A German revolution would have to be pushed forward and still forward, from stage to stage, pressing leftward, until power could be taken by the extreme left, the revolutionary proletariat. This is the concept which Marx summarized as "permanent (that is, ongoing or continuous) revolution," a revolution which does not come to a halt until the proletariat has taken power. It is this conclusion that introduced the question of proletarian power (or, same thing, proletarian 'dictatorship') into Marx's writings of 1850 analyzing the defeated revolution.[12]

3. The Fear of the 'Dictatorship' of the People

For decades Europe lay in the shadow of the defeated revolution. In the words of the *Communist Manifesto,* the ruling classes had trembled before the specter of a Communist revolution, and one of the lesser consequences fell on their mode of language. Above all, talk of the threatened (and just averted) "dictatorship" or "despotism" of the people became journalistic commonplace. Of course the idea of the "despotism of the people" goes back to Plato's and Aristotle's horror of democracy as a threat to established society; but in the 1850s this fear became pandemic.

The London *Times* thundered against giving the vote to the majority of the people on the ground that this would in effect disenfranchise "the present electors" by making the lower classes "supreme." Manchester capitalists denounced a strike as "the tyranny of Democracy." The liberal Tocqueville, writing in 1856 about the Great French Revolution, regretted that it had been carried through by "the masses on behalf of the sovereignty of the people" instead of by an "enlightened autocrat"; the revolution was a period of "popular" dictatorship, he wrote. It was perfectly clear that the "dictatorship" he lamented was the establishment of "popular sovereignty."[13]

In 1849 Guizot, the last prime minister to serve under a French king, published an interesting book, *On Democracy in France*. In a great passage, the historian-statesman complained: everyone claims to be for democracy nowadays, including monarchists and republicans as well as leftists; but democracy means chaos, class war, and popular despotism. Popular despotism means that the people impose their will over those classes which, though a minority, have the mission of ruling society. The newfangled notion that sovereignty should flow from elections is totally un-French. "Popular tyranny or military dictatorship may be the expedient of a day, but can never be a form of government."

Guizot assumed what everyone knew: democracy meant All Power to the People. This meant the dictatorship of the people. *This* dictatorship he was against.[14]

Early in the same year, a Spanish conservative became famous all over Europe for a speech made in Spain's parliament that said bluntly and even crudely what few others dared to put into words so frankly. Juan Donoso Cortés had been one of the Spanish political leaders who had helped put General Narváez into power as a virtual dictator even before the European revolution had broken out. In his "Speech on Dictatorship," Donoso had no compunction about asserting that power belonged in the hands of the propertied bourgeoisie by right of "intelligence" and by right of the saber. As for legality: "When legality suffices to save society, then legality. When it does not suffice, dictatorship." Yes, he admitted, the word 'dictatorship' is a "fearful word," but the word 'revolution' is "the most fearful of all."

It was only a question of what kind of dictatorship you favored: "it is a question of choosing between the dictatorship of the insurrection and the dictatorship of the [present] government," and *he* chose the latter. Then came his high point:

> It is a question of choosing between the dictatorship from below and the dictatorship from above: I choose the dictatorship from above, since it comes from a purer and loftier realm. It is a question of choosing, finally, between the dictatorship of the dagger and the dictatorship of the saber: I choose the dictatorship of the saber, since it is nobler.

The greatest dictatorship of all existed in England; for (mark this!) the British Parliament could do anything it wanted: "Who, gentlemen, has ever seen so colossal a dictatorship?" asked the Spanish reactionary triumphantly. It was something of an anticlimax for Donoso to reveal that God is a dictator also. This speech was quickly translated into many languages and published all over the world.[15]

At the time, less attention was given to an important book on the European revolution published in 1850 by Lorenz von Stein, who eight years before had written one of the very first studies of the burgeoning of socialism in France. Stein's analysis of "dictatorship" was complex, and cannot be summarized here; suffice it to say that he discussed it wholly in terms of class power, in particular in the context of the new proletariat's class struggles. He saw the question of "dictatorship" in terms of Louis Blanc, whom he accepted as the spokesman of the French working class.

"Social dictatorship," wrote Stein, "became the slogan of the proletariat" (meaning Blanc), "and popular representation the slogan of the Democracy and the property owners" (meaning the bourgeois democracy led by Lamartine). Louis Blanc's followers, the social-democrats, could decide to "overthrow the government, replace it exclusively by Social Democrats, and therewith establish the rule of the proletariat." The social-democrats' idea of popular sovereignty became the idea that "a Provisional Government should uphold a dictatorship until it has carried out all measures it considers necessary." "The struggle of the classes for control of the state was here clearly formulated."

Aside from the fact that he took Louis Blanc's rhetoric seriously, Stein presented the most sophisticated of the antirevolutionary analyses of the revolution. In some passages he seemed on the verge of using the very term 'dictatorship of the proletariat,' but it did not actually appear.[16]

Marx went over the same ground, in his own way, but with much the same acceptance of the current vocabulary. Like Stein, Guizot, and everyone else, he not infrequently used 'despotism' in much the same way as 'dictatorship': in combinations like "class despotism" (applied to bourgeois-democratic regimes), "parliamentary despotism," the industrial "despotism" of the factory, or the "despotic inroads on the rights of property" to be made by a workers' state. The term 'class despotism' which he used quite often in the 1850s was virtually a variation on 'class dictatorship.'[17]

In *KMTR* 3, I have made a detailed survey of how the word 'dictatorship' occurs in the writings of Marx and Engels, but the conclusion is not startling: they used the term in ways as various as everyone else did in their day, particularly in metaphorical ways, many of which are still current. They might refer to the "intellectual dictatorship" of the medieval church, or of the popes; or to a financier as "dictator" of the Crédit Mobilier. The petty states of Germany were under the "dictatorship" of Prussia or Austria; the Berlin government submitted to a "Franco-Russian dictatorship"; all Europe was under a "Muscovite dictatorship"; and just as the referee is the dictator on a soccer field, so too it was standard for the editor of a daily newspaper to be called "dictator" of the press room, even though he was subordinate to owners. Marx exercised the same "dictatorship" as editor of the Cologne daily he put out during the hectic days of revolution in 1848–49.[18]

The term 'military dictator[ship]' was less elastic; in fact, as far as I know, Marx and Engels never used this term about anyone or any regime toward which they felt kindly. I suspect this was true of the general usage too.[19]

But on the other hand, Marx applied the term 'dictator' pejoratively to a number of political figures who exercised no dictatorship at all: in these cases the term merely stressed some sort of *domination* in another form. Among these cases we find the Irish leader Parnell, Bismarck, Lord Palmerston, and a few others. This usage, fairly common in the press, should remind us of how often Franklin D. Roosevelt was called a "dictator" long after the meaning of the term had hardened.[20]

More to the point are the cases where Marx or Engels attacked efforts toward personal domination inside the working-class or socialist movement; the word 'dictatorship' was indeed apt to crop up in the denunciation. The two best cases in point are those of Bakunin and Lassalle, both seekers after personal dictatorship inside the movement, and both attacked for this reason by Marx or Engels. Bakunin's schemes for a "Secret Dictatorship" of his coterie (in the name of anarchist "libertarianism," of course) were the basis of the Bakuninists' drive to take over the International from about 1869 on; and by that time Marx came to understand that "This Russian evidently wants to become dictator of the European working-class movement." The International published a brochure written mainly by Engels and Lafargue, exposing "the organization of a secret society with the sole aim of subjecting the European workers' movement to the secret dictatorship of a few adventurers . . ." This brochure, for years derogated by unreliable historians, has been confirmed in all essential respects by the accumulation of evidence on Bakunin's dictatorial aspirations.[21]

Ferdinand Lassalle was for several years defended by Marx *against* the Communist club in the Rhineland which rejected Lassalle's bid for membership. It is now known that Lassalle did not bother to conceal his "hankerings for dictatorship" of the workers' movement, at least not from associates whom he regarded as inferiors. Marx found this out only in 1856. Then in an 1862 visit to Marx, Lassalle revealed more of his dictatorial ideas, his hostility to "individual liberty," and his propensity for behaving "as if he were the future workers' dictator." Marx told him that they were poles apart, agreeing "on nothing except some far-distant ultimate ends," and chaffed him as an "enlightened Bonapartist." The accuracy of this assessment was fully confirmed when research turned up Lassalle's attempt in 1863 to use the newly organized Lassallean social-democratic organization to make a deal with Bismarck: the Lassallean socialists would support a "social dictatorship" by the Crown in exchange for concessions. In this letter Lassalle pointed to his own personal "dictatorship" in the organization as evidence of the willingness of the "working class" to support dictatorship. The general nature of Lassalle's machinations with Bismarck were known in the movement at the time, and were reported to Marx. It is hard to see why the myth of Marx's "personal" hatred for Lassalle had to be invented to account for hostility to a man with such politics.[22]

In a number of other cases Marx expressed his opinion on efforts at *personal* dictatorship in the movement. Of Auguste Comte, whose sect called itself Positivist and was active in working-class circles, Marx wrote that he was a "prophet" of "personal *Dictatorship*"—"author of a new catechism with a new pope and new saints." In England, where H. M. Hyndman founded a self-styled Marxist group, the Social Democratic Federation, his dictatorial conduct as boss of the organization was notorious. Hyndman, wrote Engels, had alienated associates particularly by "his impatience to play the dictator." In what was left of the Chartist movement by 1855, Ernest Jones thought to stem decay by concentrating all organizational power in his own hands. Marx wrote the news to Engels that Jones "has proclaimed himself dictator of Chartism," stirred a storm of indignation against himself, and showed himself an "ass" in his effort "to play the dictator himself."[23]

These examples of the use of 'dictatorship' indicate the spectrum of meaning common in the nineteenth century. Indeed, much of this spectrum still conditions the term today; metaphorical uses are still common. But when Marx first wrote down the term 'dictatorship of the proletariat,' it was a very specific sort of metaphorical usage.

4. 'Dictatorship of the Proletariat': First Period

Quite early, by 1844, Marx came to the conclusion that, to achieve a communist transformation of society, the proletariat first had to conquer political power. This idea played a basic role for him, and various terms expressing it dot his writings: not only 'conquest of political (*or* state) power,' but 'rule of the proletariat' in particular; the outcome would be a 'workers' state'; in terms of the British movement, this meant 'proletarian ascendancy.' We are going to see that, under given circumstances, one of these terms was *also* going to be 'dictatorship of the proletariat.'[24]

Marx recognized that this aim, the political 'rule of the proletariat,' was not at all unique to his own theory; on the contrary, he liked to stress that *all* other real working-class movements set this as their goal. This is strongly stated in the *Communist Manifesto:*[25]

> The immediate aim of the Communists is the same as that of all the other proletarian parties: constitution of the proletariat into a class, overthrow of bourgeois rule, conquest of political power by the proletariat.

Above all, Marx knew and appreciated that the left Chartists (e.g., Harney) regularly advocated the "ascendancy" (or rule, or political power) of the proletariat.[26] These Chartists, like Marx, had no trouble with the alleged problem raised by modern marxologists: *How can a whole class rule?* The answer was the same for Marx and the Chartists as it was for their opponents, for (say) the liberal historian Macaulay, who feared universal suffrage on the ground that it would put "supreme power" in the hands of a class, the class of labor, hence generating a "despotism," by which he openly meant a despotism over the bourgeoisie.[27]

We are going to see, then, that Marx used the term 'dictatorship of the proletariat' in exactly the same way as he used 'rule of the proletariat' and the other labels for a workers' state. But under what circumstances did he tend to do so? A major clue is found in the fact that Marx's and Engels' use of the term 'dictatorship of the proletariat' clustered in three periods and was in fact notably absent in-between. These three periods were the following:

> Period I: 1850 to 1852, the postrevolutionary period after the upheaval of 1848–1849.
> Period II: 1871 to 1875, the postrevolutionary period after the Paris Commune.
> Period III (naturally involving Engels only): a sort of echo from 1875.[28]

In view of the career of the word 'dictatorship,' there is now no very difficult problem about Marx's willingness to replace 'rule' with 'dictatorship' in certain contexts. But a review of these contexts is enlightening.

Locus 1. In the first chapter of his *Class Struggles in France,* Marx mentioned that in the course of the revolution in France, "there appeared the bold slogan of revolutionary struggle: *Overthrow of the bourgeoisie! Dictatorship of the working class!*" Since there is absolutely no record that "dictatorship of the proletariat" appeared as a slogan at all, I suggest that Marx is not saying here that *it* appeared; he is only placing it in apposition with the slogan that did appear, the first-mentioned slogan, namely "Overthrow of the bourgeoisie!" In effect he is explaining what the first-mentioned slogan meant. In the same passage, by the way, Marx freely used "bourgeois terrorism" and "bourgeois dictatorship" interchangeably with bourgeois "rule" to characterize the "bourgeois republic."[29]

In the second chapter, Marx mentioned that the proletariat was not yet sufficiently developed to take power itself: "the proletariat . . . [was] not yet enabled through the development of the remaining classes to seize the revolutionary dictatorship . . ." In writing this, Marx, as often, excluded the idea of a seizure of power by a minority in the Blanquist fashion.[30]

In the third chapter (written in March 1850 and published in April) Marx dissected the pink socialism of Louis Blanc and reported that as against such social-democratic reform currents, "the *proletariat* increasingly organizes itself around *revolutionary socialism,* around *com-*

munism, for which the bourgeoisie itself has invented the name of *Blanqui.*" It is important to note what this clearly states: Blanqui's name was inventively applied to the communist tendency by its enemies, the bourgeoisie—and not by Marx himself.[31]

Marx's chapter goes on to say that this revolutionary socialism "is the *declaration of the permanence of the revolution,* the *class dictatorship* of the proletariat as the necessary transit point to the *abolition of class distinctions generally*" and thence to the revolutionizing of all society. Please note that Marx's emphasis is on the term 'class dictatorship.'

Marx's reference to Blanqui is a shorthand reference to the then well-known use of Blanqui's name as a revolutionary bogey by the counterrevolutionary politicians. At a crucial point in April 1848, when a workers' demonstration against the government was building up, the right-wing Provisional Government leaders organized a massive campaign to circulate the story that Blanqui and his friends were preparing to overthrow the government and take over. (One of the first well-organized "red scares.")

KMTR 3 gives some space to Louis Blanc's own historical account of the use made of Blanqui's "name as a sort of bugbear." Blanc referred to "the part so cleverly assigned to M. Blanqui, the better to frighten the bourgeoisie"—a role assigned, or invented, by the government majority anxious to put an end to revolutionary pressure from below. This is the meaning of Marx's reference to the communist bugbear "for which the bourgeoisie itself has invented the name of Blanqui."[32]

The repeated claim that in this passage Marx was himself equating the 'dictatorship of the proletariat' phrase with Blanqui is a remarkable distortion that is almost standard among marxologists, not infrequently based on outright mistranslation.[33]

Locus 2. In April 1850 the phrase 'dictatorship of the proletariat' again cropped up, *in connection with* the Blanquists but not as their expression.

At this time, still expecting that the quiescent revolution would burst out again on the Continent, Marx and his comrades of the Communist League, in London exile, looked for cooperative relations with other revolutionary groups. One of these was the left wing of the Chartists, led by Harney, already in close touch with Marx's circle. Among the French, the only group Marx considered to be revolutionary was the Blanquist tendency, which had no prominent leaders and few ideas but did have some influence in the émigré community. Talks took place among these three tendencies looking toward the establishment of a sort of united-front organization for revolutionary cooperation. A number of programmatic points were jotted down—not by Marx or Engels—for consideration under the heading "Société Universelle des Communistes Révolutionnaires."*

All we really know of SUCR is that some sort of preliminary agreement was reached to discuss this proposal. All the participants signed the paper with the programmatic points. There is no evidence that any organization resulted. Indeed all the evidence indicates that the idea remained strictly on paper and never got off the ground. By October Marx—who had meanwhile come to the conclusion that the revolutionary situation was over for that period—repudiated the SUCR project.[34]

For what it is worth, then, we can report that the SUCR program set down this article first of all: "The aim of the association is the downfall of all the privileged classes, to subject these classes to the dictatorship of the proletarians, maintaining the revolution in permanence until the realization of communism . . ."[35]

The "dictatorship of the proletarians" is a formula that Marx never used elsewhere; this is only one of several reasons to believe that the program was drafted not by Marx but by August Willich, a member of the Communist League close to the Blanquists personally.[36] There is no mystery about why this phrase, as well as "revolution in permanence," appealed to these people. The attractive appeal of these terms to Blanquist types who did not understand their content suggests a hypothesis on why, and under what circumstances, Marx occasionally used the term 'dictatorship of the proletariat.'[37]

The same hypothesis explains why the term makes its appearance *in connection with* the Blanquists but not *by* the Blanquists. Ordinarily Marx's term for the idea would be, as we have seen, 'rule of the proletariat,' 'political power of the working class,' etc. *But when it is a question of counterposing this class concept to the Blanquist-type dictatorship, it is dressed in the formula 'class dictatorship.'* Class dictatorship is then counterposed to Blanquist dictatorship, to make the contrast.

---

*The full story of SUCR is set out for the first time in Chapter 12 of *KMTR* 3, which gives particular attention to the myths spun about SUCR by such writers as Nicolaievsky.

Particularly in united fronts with the Blanquists, it was only such a formulation that would be acceptable to Marx. On its basis he could undertake to do what was necessary to re-educate his partners. Joint collaboration with these partners took place on a formulation that preserved the class character that was fundamental for Marx, while at the same time no doubt making the Blanquists happy with its revolutionary flavor.

To understand this, the reader must put aside the modern aura that makes 'dictatorship' a dirty word for us; for this aura did not yet exist. How do you counteract the primitive notion of dictatorship that was so common precisely among the people who wanted to be good revolutionaries? You tell them: *Dictatorship? That means rule. Yes, we want the rule of the proletariat; but that does not mean the rule of a man or a clique or a band or a party; it means the rule of a class.* Class rule means *class* dictatorship.

This is how the term came from Marx's pen in 1850: an instrument in the re-education of the Blanquist and Jacobin-revolutionary currents around Marx's own circle. The marxological myth which had 'dictatorship of the proletariat' pegged as a "Blanquist" idea had history turned upside-down. 'Dictatorship of the proletariat' came into existence as an attempt to show would-be revolutionaries that there was *another* way of being revolutionary, Marx's way.

This understood, we can restate our basic thesis on the meaning of the term *to Marx*. For Marx and Engels, from beginning to end of their careers and without exception, 'dictatorship of the proletariat' meant nothing more and nothing less than 'rule of the proletariat'— the 'conquest of political power' by the working class, the establishment of a workers' state in the immediate postrevolutionary period.[38]

The subsequent career of the term provides proof after proof of this thesis; at the same time no evidence turns up to gainsay it. This is the claim to be tested in the light of the facts.

5. The First Period—Continued

The next appearances of the 'dictatorship of the proletariat' were echoes from Locus 1.

Locus 3. Otto Lüning, the socialistic editor of a leftist paper in

Frankfurt, wrote a four-installment review of Marx's *N.R.Z. Revue* articles on *The Class Struggles in France*. It was published in June in Lüning's *Neue Deutsche Zeitung*.[39] What Lüning criticized above all was the "red thread" that wound through Marx's conception of society and history: "the cleavage of present-day society into different classes" with contradictory interests. Lüning's kind of socialism believed in class harmony and reform. He therefore repeatedly underlined that Marx advocated the taking of political power by the working class: for Marx the aim of the revolutionary movement is "the *revolutionary rule, the dictatorship of the working class*." But what Lüning keeps attacking is the "rule." He finally reveals that his sharpest disagreement is with Marx's emphasis on "the transference of rule from one class to another" *instead* of on "the destruction of class differences."

At no point did Lüning indicate any special interest in the term 'dictatorship of the proletariat,' which he himself mentioned in passing. Throughout he was intent on repudiating the aim of a working-class state, of class rule, as well as (later in his review) attacking the very idea of a class interpretation of history. Obviously Lüning's views had a great future as the format for anti-Marxism, but it was not 'dictatorship of the proletariat' that drew blood.[40]

Marx, who at first intended to write a longer analysis of Lüning for the *N.R.Z. Revue*, compromised on a letter to the editor in the latter's paper. Marx's letter was short and sententious and replied only to Lüning's claim that Marx had written *only* about 'rule of the proletariat' and not about the further aim of abolishing class differences. It referred to the charge about "the rule and the dictatorship of the working class" but, just like Lüning, was interested only in the "rule" idea. The letter listed a series of references and citations to Marx's writings in which the "abolition of class differences" had been prominently discussed, including the very passage that Lüning was reviewing.[41]

What stands out, in Marx's letter as in Lüning's attack, was that the term 'dictatorship of the proletariat' was *not* specially involved—for either of them. Both assumed that it had no special content other than 'rule of the proletariat.'

Locus 4. Lüning's associate editor and brother-in-law was a good friend and comrade of Marx's, Joseph Weydemeyer. In 1851 Weydemeyer had to flee government harassment in Germany, and finally decided to emigrate to the United States. Soon after his arrival in November, he began writing for the radical German-American press, while corresponding with Marx. His first article appeared in the New York *Turn-Zeitung* for January 1, 1852, an issue which also offered the first installment of Engels' *Peasant War in Germany* as well as Weydemeyer's announcement of his own forthcoming weekly.[42]

The title of Weydemeyer's article was "Die Diktatur des Proletariats" (The Dictatorship of the Proletariat). The article was solely concerned with the subject of the *rule* of the working class as expounded in the *Communist Manifesto,* which is the source of the contents of the piece. The term in the title is not even repeated in the body of the article until the last passage, which speaks of the need for any revolution to have "a dictatorship at its head," and then presents the idea of the dictatorship of "the proletariat which is concentrated in the big cities," not the proletariat *tout court.* Obviously Weydemeyer did not grasp the idea of a class dictatorship, however many times Marx had underlined that term.

Now as he wrote an article condensing the teachings of the Manifesto (as was clearly Weydemeyer's aim), why did the title term occur to him? The answer, not very conjectural, is that he had only recently stood close on the sidelines as his associate Lüning had lifted a lance against "the rule, the dictatorship of the working class."[43]

Marx must have recently received a copy of Weydemeyer's article (though there is no record of this) when on March 5, 1852, in response to his friend's letters, Marx wrote him a lengthy bit of advice on how to deal with issues in the German-American press. It was in this context that Marx criticized the refusal by writers like Karl Heinzen to recognize the existence of classes in society. Marx wrote that no credit was due to him for discovering the existence of classes in modern society or the class struggle among them.

> What I did that was new was (1) to show that the *existence of classes* is simply bound up with *certain historical phases of the development of production;* (2) that the class struggle necessarily leads to the *dictatorship of the proletariat;* (3) that this dictatorship itself only constitutes the transition to the *abolition of all classes* and to a *classless society.*

If the reader substitutes the usual 'rule of the proletariat' for the striking phrase here, the content of this statement will be perfectly clear. There is nothing whatever in this passage to indicate that Marx thought he was making an unusual pronouncement. Then why did he use 'dictatorship of the proletariat' instead of his usual term? Well, this is precisely what is explained by the fact that Weydemeyer himself had just given that term special visibility. Marx's letter was simply echoing the title of the article by Weydemeyer, who was himself echoing the recent exchange in the *NDZ* between Marx and Lüning. Marx was throwing in a phrase that had special associations for his correspondent. Writing a personal letter, Marx could let this be understood. When taken out of this context and held up to view as if it were an extraordinary statement, its significance is distorted.[44]

6. The Second Period of 'Dictatorship of the Proletariat'

In the two decades before the Paris Commune, there was not a single case of Marx's use of 'dictatorship of the proletariat.'[45] As always, he kept referring to the 'rule of the proletariat,' 'conquest of political power,' 'workers' state,' and similar expressions to denote the assumption of state power by the working class. Accidental? It is entirely explainable in terms of the thesis offered above. During these two decades, in which the left movement was at a low ebb, Marx's work and activities did not involve him in any connection with Blanquist elements. There was no need for him to deal with their conception of dictatorship.

For the same reason the term 'dictatorship of the proletariat' did not appear in *The Civil War in France,* the defense and analysis of the Paris Commune that Marx wrote for the General Council of the International. At this time, and until the Communard refugees started trickling into London, the Blanquists had refused any ties with the International; it was not "revolutionary" enough for them.

In *The Civil War in France* Marx argued that the Commune was a "working-class government," "the political form at last discovered under which to work out the economical emancipation of Labour." The Commune was a *workers' state* of brief duration and naturally with all kinds of limitations and inadequacies. Marx's characterization of the Commune was so sweeping in this regard that there can be no doubt that, for him, it was accepted as an example of the *rule* (or "dictatorship") of the proletariat.

At the same time *The Civil War in France* filled pages with a description and celebration of the extraordinary advance in *democracy* repre-sented by the Commune government form and actions. The Commune "supplied the Republic with the basis of really democratic institutions"; its measures "could but betoken the tendency of a gov-ernment of the people by the people."[46]

It is clear that, in Marx's eyes, the Commune took no "dictatorial" measures—if the present-day meaning of the word is used. Indeed there had been a proposal inside the Commune to do just that, as the military situation grew more and more precarious before the military power of the Versailles government. The Blanquist-Jacobin majority of the Commune proposed to set up a dictatorial body to be called (shades of Robespierre) a Committee of Public Safety, with special arbitrary powers. The debate over "dictatorship" (this is how it was put) was acrimonious; when the proposal was adopted, the Minority walked out of the Commune. This split would have attracted more attention from historians than it has if the final Versaillese assault on the city had not commenced at virtually the moment of the split, making it academic as all pitched in to the military defense. But in hindsight it is important to note that the antidictatorial Minority represented most of the International people as well as the Proudhonists, and in particular it included all the figures who had any special connection with Marx or showed any tendency to look to his ideas (for example, Serraillier, who was practically Marx's personal representative; Frankel, Longuet, Varlin).[47]

Since the Paris Commune clearly had no "dictatorial" trappings in the modern sense, it has always represented a problem for those who maintain that Marx's 'dictatorship of the proletariat' meant something specially "dictatorial" as compared with a mere workers' state. When we find that Marx (not only Engels) had no compunction about calling it a "dictatorship of the proletariat," this fact itself speaks volumes about our basic thesis.

After the fall of the Commune, Blanquist Communards among others found their way to London, where they began working with Marx, especially on refugee aid; several were co-opted onto the Gen-eral Council. No evidence is needed to understand that Marx naturally discussed his views with them, as with others; but there is good evidence nevertheless. In other words, as in the 1850s, Marx tried to "re-educate" them from his standpoint.[48] The Blanquists just as natu-rally set out to turn the International into a Blanquist sect. With this two-way influence, it is of the greatest interest that *now* we find Marx—once again after twenty years—using the term 'dictatorship of the proletariat.' And we will also now find the Blanquist refugees using it too!—in their case, for the first time.[49]

Locus 5. The first post-Commune meeting of the International was the London Conference of September 1871. At its end there was an anniversary celebration of the International's founding, bringing the participants together in a social occasion—a banquet plus "toasts" (short speeches). Marx was voted into the chair and forced to make a short speech.

A correspondent of the *New York World* sent in a longish dispatch about the banquet ("The Reds in Session") with a considerable summary of Marx's talk. About the Commune, Marx reiterated his view that "the Commune was the conquest of the political power of the working classes." Its aim was to remove any "base for class rule and oppression": "But before such a change could be effected a proletarian dictature would become necessary . . ." (The verbs are those of the reporter's paraphrase.)

Thus Marx's first use of the term since 1852 took place before an assemblage heavily weighted with Blanquist Communards, where "the name that set the whole assembly in motion like an electric shock was Blanqui's" (in the words of the dispatch). Apparently Marx even used the French form of the term *(dictature)*. He was once again confronting the Blanquist mind with his own conception of *class* dictatorship.[50]

Locus 6. Marx's next use of the term came in an article written around the turn of the year 1872 into 1873, as a polemic against Proudhon and anarchism, not so much on anarchism itself as on the anarchist stance of principled hostility to revolutionary political activity. It was published in December 1873 in an Italian socialist annual under the title "Indifference to Politics."

The article begins abruptly with a long section, all in quotation marks, which purports to represent what an antipolitical Proudhonist or anarchist would say if he set down his views frankly. The 'dictatorship' term occurs in the course of this fictitious speech; for the speaker is shown attacking the idea of the 'dictatorship of the proletariat' in the same way as he attacks any idea of political action or political power.

In this way the Proudhonist is represented as asserting: "If the political struggle of the working class assumes violent forms, if the workers substitute their revolutionary dictatorship for the dictatorship of the bourgeois class, they commit the terrible crime of violating principle . . ." For (continues Marx) the workers do not lay down arms and abolish the state but rather "give it a revolutionary and transitional form."

As usual, the 'dictatorship' phrase is used here as only another formulation for workers' political power; but there is a special interest. Here Marx makes the thought plain by counterposing two class "dictatorships"; the "dictatorship of the bourgeois class" is made coordinate with the "revolutionary dictatorship" of the working class. This usage underlines that Marx thinks of class dictatorships (either one) in terms of the class nature of political power, rather than in terms of special governmental forms.[51]

When the Hague Congress of the International (September 1872) decided to transfer the center to New York—a proposal Marx made, no doubt, in order to stave off the coming push by the Blanquists to take over the movement for their own purposes, having helped save it from Bakunin—the Blanquists reacted by announcing their split from the International and their open reconstitution of a Blanquist sect. By this time their programmatic ideas had undergone a degree of "Marxification," though not on their basic notion of revolution by a putschist band. In pamphlets, *Internationale et Révolution* (1872) and *Aux Communeux* (1874), they set down their ideas. As Engels wrote to a friend, the 1872 brochure "quite seriously explains all our economic and political principles as Blanquist discoveries." This is a jocular exaggeration, but indeed the Blanquists threw in the term 'dictatorship of the proletariat' as a new formulation (new for them) for the coming Blanquist seizure of power.* This led to Engels' first use of the term under his own name.[52]

Locus 7. Hard on the heels of Marx's Italian article, Engels used the term in Part III of his work *The Housing Question*. It occurred in two passages.

---

*The passages in the Blanquist brochures which talked about "dictatorship" are quoted and discussed in *KMTR* 3; they would be digressive here. Suffice it to say that other passages in the brochures still made it clear that, however new their phraseology, they still advocated the assumption of revolutionary power by a minority band, in the traditional Blanquist sense.

In the first Engels discussed the Blanquist pamphlet of 1872, which, he claimed, "adopted, and almost literally at that, the views of German scientific socialism on the necessity of political action by the proletariat and of its dictatorship as the transition to the abolition of classes and with them of the state—views such as had already been expressed in the *Communist Manifesto* and since then on innumerable occasions." This shows strikingly that Engels saw nothing in the term 'dictatorship of the proletariat' which was not already in, say, the Manifesto—which said nothing about any "dictatorship."

The second passage is interesting for a similar reason. Here Engels was polemizing against a Proudhonist, who attacked the very notion of class political power, or "class rule." Engels replies: why, *every* political party wants to establish its rule in the state; a socialist workers' party likewise strives for the rule of the working class.

> Moreover, *every* real proletarian party, from the English Chartists onward, has always put forward a class policy, the organization of the proletariat as an independent political party, as the first condition of the struggle, and the dictatorship of the proletariat as the immediate aim of the struggle.

What leaps to the eye is Engels' assumption that 'dictatorship of the proletariat' has no *special* meaning other than the establishment of the "rule" of the working class. "Every" real working-class party stands for it: this statement can make no sense to anyone who believes that there is some special "theory of proletarian dictatorship" in Marx and Engels, involving special notions about "dictatorial" measures.[53]

Locus 8. The clearest explanation of the meaning of 'dictatorship of the proletariat' came soon (1874) in an article by Engels devoted precisely to the Blanquists' adoption of the term, in their brochure *Aux Communeux.* This article, "Program of the Blanquist Refugees of the Commune," is, far and away, the best analysis of the Blanquist tendency ever published, but this is not our present subject. Its statement on *our* subject goes as follows:

> From the fact that Blanqui conceives of every revolution as the *coup de main* of a small revolutionary minority, what follows of itself is the necessity of dictatorship after its success—the dictatorship, please note, not of the entire revolutionary class, the proletariat, but of the small number of those who made the *coup de main* and who themselves are organized beforehand under the dictatorship of one person or a few.
>
> One can see that Blanqui is a revolutionary of the previous generation.

There could be no more instructive differentiation between—on the one hand—Marx's conception of the 'dictatorship of the proletariat' as the rule ('dictatorship') of a majority class or class movement, and—on the other—the traditional conception of dictatorship, the idea of the "previous generation," as the dictatorship of the party or revolutionary band, hence entailing the dictatorship of the latter *over* the proletariat.[54]

Locus 9. The confrontation with the Blanquists, we see, produced several contexts for the 'dictatorship of the proletariat' during the first half of the 1870s. The term had cropped up, and this no doubt accounts for the fact that it was used by Marx in an important document in 1875.

As the two German socialist parties—the so-called "Eisenachers" led by Bebel and the Lassalleans—prepared to unite at a congress in Gotha, a draft program made for the occasion was filled with concessions to the Lassalleans. Marx, incensed, sent a letter to Eisenacher leaders, critically analyzing the program and attacking the Lassallean formulations and ideas. This "Critique of the Gotha Program" was neither a personal letter nor a public article, but a restricted circular of political discussion.

The passage referring to 'dictatorship of the proletariat' is one of the most often-quoted loci, but also one of the barest. It came in a section where Marx first attacked the Lassallean formula "free state." No, wrote Marx, we do not want to make the state "free," but rather to put it under democratic control. "Freedom consists in transforming the state from an organ set above society into one thoroughly subordinated to it, and today too the state forms are more free or less free to the extent that they restrict the 'freedom of the state.'" This was a blow struck against "the Lassallean sect's servile belief in the state." Marx next objected to confusing the terms "present-day state" and "present-day society." The latter is capitalist society, and *different* present-day states may have capitalist society as their social basis. He then raised a question about the "future" state beyond bourgeois society:

> The question comes up, then: what transformation will the state undergo in a communist society? In other words, what societal functions will remain there that are analogous to the present state functions?

His answer was lamentably brief:

Between the capitalist and the communist society lies the period of the revolutionary transformation of the one into the other. To this there corresponds a political transition period whose state can be nothing but *the revolutionary dictatorship of the proletariat.*

The one thing this short statement makes clear is that Marx did not think in terms of more or less dictatorial forms of the transitional period represented by the workers' state. Especially in the twentieth century it was not uncommon to read that, according to Marx, a workers' state might *or might not* be a "dictatorship of the proletariat," depending presumably on how severely dictatorial it had to become. This interpretation is excluded by Marx's words: the workers' state "can be nothing but" a dictatorship of the proletariat; in other words, the two terms are synonymous. In this connection, it is worth noting that, soon after the passage quoted, Marx warned against confusing the "state" with the "government machine." This has to be applied to the previous statement that in the transitional period the *state* will be the dictatorship of the proletariat. For Marx this was a statement about the societal content of the state, the class character of the political power. It was not a statement about the forms of the government machine or other structural aspects of government or policies.[55]

This was the last appearance of 'dictatorship of the proletariat' in Marx's writings.

7. *The Third Period of 'Dictatorship of the Proletariat'*

When Marx died in 1883, the term had not come up for eight years; and another seven years passed before it appeared again under Engels' name. During this fifteen-year hiatus, the old Blanquist problem that had originally elicited the term had completely changed. When the term re-emerged, it was as an echo from 1875, that is, it was due to the publication of Marx's "Critique of the Gotha Program."

In 1890 the German Social-Democratic Party was preparing to adopt a new party program, replacing the Gotha Program of 1875. (The new program was going to be adopted by the Erfurt Congress of 1891.) Engels was determined to use the pre-Congress discussion to make known to the movement what the party leadership (specifically

Liebknecht, Bebel being in prison) had done its best to suppress, namely Marx's views on Lassalle and Lassalleanism. Engels disinterred the manuscript from Marx's papers and, with some difficulty, managed to get it published in the party press.[56]

Locus 10. In October 1890, as he was pulling the critique out of the archive, he sat down to write a letter to a comrade discussing the materialist conception of history. This is one of the letters in which Engels explained that this conception does *not* present economic factors as alone operative in history. Look at Marx's *Eighteenth Brumaire,* he advised, "which almost exclusively concerns itself with the *special* role that political struggles and events play, naturally within the framework of their *general* dependence on economic conditions." Pointing to other analyses by Marx, he added:

> Or why then do we fight for the political dictatorship of the proletariat, if political power is economically powerless? Force (i.e., state power) is also an economic power. [Letter to C. Schmidt, October 27, 1890]

Once again, we see, Engels assumed, as a matter that did not even require discussion, that 'dictatorship of the proletariat' was a mere synonym for the conquest of political power by the working class. Once again, if the term is assigned a narrower or more special meaning, this rather casual reference by Engels ceases to make sense.[57]

When Marx's "Critique" was published in the *Neue Zeit,* it was a "bombshell" (as Engels said). The main reason for this was its criticism of Lassalleanism, but the reference to the "revolutionary dictatorship of the proletariat" was equally denounced by the right wing of the party. One leader of the parliamentary group repudiated it on the floor of the Reichstag. For a while the entire party leadership boycotted Engels personally for daring to make Marx's views known to the party membership and the public. Never before had the right wing's hostility to Marx come out in the open as it did now.[58]

Locus 11. Meanwhile Engels was working on a new edition of Marx's *The Civil War in France.* In March he finished his new introduction to that analysis of the Paris Commune. This was in effect an essay on the Commune: once more he dissected the Blanquist approach to revolution—

> the viewpoint that a relatively small number of resolute, well-organized men would be able . . . to maintain power until they succeeded in sweeping the mass of people into the revolution and ranging them round

the small band of leaders. This involved, above all, the strictest, dictatorial centralization of all power in the hands of the new revolutionary government.

Like Marx, Engels reviewed the Commune's implementation of real democracy. And then, at the very end, he paid his respects to the right-wingers who were attacking Marx's "Critique":

> Of late, the Social-Democratic philistine has once more been filled with wholesome terror at the phrase: dictatorship of the proletariat. Well and good, gentlemen, do you want to know what this dictatorship looks like? Look at the Paris Commune. That was the dictatorship of the proletariat.

In calling the Commune a 'dictatorship of the proletariat' Engels was echoing Marx's banquet speech of 1871, which until quite recently was virtually unknown to the marxological industry. Hence for a very long time it was customary for writers to assert that this was Engels' own invention—for how could the Commune be a 'dictatorship of the proletariat' if it did not take some sturdily "dictatorial" steps? Plainly these marxologists will have to argue that Marx—like Engels—did not understand "Marxism"; only they do, having virtually invented it.[59]

Locus 12. Three months later, Engels had another bombshell ready for the "Social-Democratic philistine" wing of the party: a critique of the draft Erfurt Program. He was taking the opportunity, he said, "to strike at the peaceable opportunism of the *Vorwärts* [the party organ]" and at the reformist view that bourgeois society would of itself "grow" into socialist society. (By the way, the myth that by this time Engels had become an advocate of "peaceable" gradualism was invented, after his death, by the very people against whom this campaign was directed.)

Engels' critique of the draft program especially raised the question of including a demand for the democratic republic as one of the "democratic" planks, and argued that a peaceful assumption of power was not possible in Germany. This emphasis was directed head-on against the trend toward reformist adaptation to the German imperial state which was developing in the party. He wrote:

> If anything is established, it is that our party and the working class can come to power only under the form of the democratic republic. This is even the specific form for the dictatorship of the proletariat, as the great French revolution [the Paris Commune] has already shown.

It was another chance for Engels to get in a lick for the phrase that had recently upset all the Social-Democratic philistines; in a different year he might have said, "specific form for the workers' state." But the important thing was that he was explaining the relationship between the *governmental form* (democratic republic) and the class content of the state (dictatorship of the proletariat). The Paris Commune⋆ had shown in revolutionary practice that a workers' state (dictatorship of the proletariat) could and probably would be based on the forms of the democratic republic.[61]

Engels' coupling of 'dictatorship of the proletariat' with the term 'democratic republic' has been another target for the marxological campaign to turn 'dictatorship of the proletariat' into a special slogan about dictatorship. Much of this campaign depends, unwittingly, on the *later* pattern according to which the term 'democratic' was used as a shorthand form for 'bourgeois-democratic,' especially but not only in the Russian movement. But neither Marx nor Engels ever *limited* the word 'democratic' to the meaning of 'bourgeois-democratic.' Indeed, no one has ever tried to show that they did; we are again dealing with an unthought-through assumption, based on the naive belief that one's own political jargon had arisen with Adam.

But the main difficulty has not been inability to see that 'democratic republic,' to most people, meant a republic that was democratic, and not some special term that only the sophisticated initiates could understand. The main difficulty, as before, is the assumption that a 'dictatorship of the proletariat' *has* to be "dictatorial" in the modern sense, and therefore could not be clothed in straightforward democratic forms.[62]

Engels, who thought that a 'democratic republic' meant a democratic republic, had a proposal to make in his critique of the draft Erfurt Program, especially for those who argued that the demand for a democratic republic could not be openly placed in the program because the government would utilize it as a pretext to harass the party. We can get around that, he suggested: "in my opinion what should go

---

⋆Because of the expression "great French revolution," the assumption has often been made that Engels meant the French Revolution of 1789; but the idea that he, or anyone else, could view 1789 (or 1793) as a 'dictatorship of the proletariat' is too absurd to entertain. The specific reasons why this interpretation is untenable are presented in *KMTR* 3.[60]

in and can go in is the demand for the *concentration of all political power in the hands of the people's representation.*" This is a classic formulation of the meaning of thoroughgoing democracy: "the concentration of all political power in the hands of the people's representation." It would stand for the illegal "democratic republic," which is "the specific form for the dictatorship of the proletariat." Engels, the advocate of that revolutionary dictatorship which so appalled the right wing, was arguing with them that they should say something about their goal of a democratic republic *instead of adapting themselves to the legality of the kaiser's regime.*[63]

8. *Engels vs. Plekhanov: Pointer to the Future*

The last echo of 'dictatorship of the proletariat' that comes to us from Engels' last years points straight ahead to the next period, in which the term parted company with Marx and Engels.

In 1893 a young Russian Social-Democratic émigré visited Engels. Plekhanov, the leader and theoretician of the relatively new Russian Marxist group, had given him a letter of recommendation. A third of a century later, A. M. Voden wrote up his memoirs, including his "Talks with Engels."

Just why 'dictatorship of the proletariat' came into the conversation is not clear from Voden's account. The two were discussing the relations between Narodniks (Russian Populists) and the Russian Social-Democrats, including Plekhanov's attitude. Voden writes:

> Engels asked how Plekhanov himself stood on the question of the dictatorship of the proletariat. I was forced to admit that G. V. Plekhanov had repeatedly expressed his conviction to me that when "we" come to power, of course "we" would allow freedom to no one but "ourselves" . . . However, in response to my question who exactly should be taken to be the monopolists of freedom, Plekhanov answered: the working class headed by comrades who correctly understand Marx's teachings and who draw the correct conclusions from those teachings. And in response to my question on what comprises the objective criteria for a correct understanding of Marx's teachings and the correct practical conclusions flowing therefrom, G. V. Plekhanov limited himself to the statement that it was all laid out "clearly enough, it seems" in his (Plekhanov's) works.

If Voden's report was accurate (and there is no reason to doubt it), then it is clear what the leader and teacher of Russian Social-Democracy—destined also to be the leading theoretician of Russian Menshevism—was teaching his movement. When "we" seize power, democratic rights ("freedom") would be withdrawn from opponents, and a dictatorial regime would be imposed with the dictatorship in the hands of the victorious party or just its leadership. There is no mystery about where Plekhanov—himself a Narodnik only a few years before—had gotten these notions: this conception of dictatorship had long been the unquestioned orthodoxy of the Blanquist and Bakuninist elements who had long provided most of the training of Russian (and other) revolutionaries. He did not get it *from* Marx's old term; the relationship was the other way 'round—this was the standard conception which he imposed on Marx's term when he heard it.

And what did Engels think of this, when told by Voden? We learn this in Voden's memoirs, which continue as follows:

> After inquiring whether I personally on the other hand was satisfied with such an objective criterion [that is, Plekhanov's], Engels expressed the opinion that the application of that sort of criterion would either lead to the Russian Social-Democracy's turning into a sect with its unavoidable and always undesirable practical consequences, or it would give rise in the Russian Social-Democracy—at least among the émigré Russian Social-Democrats—to a series of splits from which Plekhanov himself would not benefit.

In short, thought Engels, Plekhanov's perspective would wreck the movement, either by a split or (what amounts to the same thing) sectification. There is an indication in Voden's memoirs that there was more to report about Engels' hostile reception to this account of the Russian leader's views. Engels remarked that Plekhanov seemed to him a Russian analogue of H. M. Hyndman. Voden footnoted that Plekhanov took this as a compliment, and it is likely that Voden had no idea of what it meant. Hyndman, the leader of the British "Marxist" sect which Marx and Engels used to denounce in the most cutting terms, was furthermore viewed by them as a sect *dictator,* whose dictatorial patterns had split the movement more than once.

It is hard to exaggerate the significance of this little-known episode, as a symbol and as an educational beam of light on the meaning of the question. In just a few years the Russian Social-Democratic Workers Party was going to become the first socialist organization in the world to include the 'dictatorship of the proletariat' in its program—though Marx and Engels had always refused to propose such a step. The term was written into the party program by Plekhanov, who by that time was perhaps the most prestigious theoretician of Marxism outside Germany.[64]

Thus the new era of the 'dictatorship of the proletariat' was launched on its way—not by Lenin (as the usual myth has it) but by the future leader and theoretician of Menshevism.

Thus the antidemocratic interpretation of 'dictatorship of the proletariat,' repudiated by Engels when it was reported to him, was going to blossom in the Second International and particularly in the Russian movement.

2
Second International Sketches (Still Life)

We have seen, and will see again to a much greater degree, that Marx's term 'dictatorship of the proletariat' was misunderstood. Misunderstood? This fact is something that itself needs to be understood.

Marx's and Engels' letters to each other made this complaint more than once: their own followers had failed to understand what they were teaching. The complaints were usually quite justified, but the phenomenon itself requires a deeper analysis than mere disgust with the disciples' lack of understanding. Not very deep, in fact on the surface, was a big factor that marxologists tend to overlook, as they focus only on the relations between disciple and teacher. *The disciples were always more heavily influenced by their own environments, socialist and capitalist, than by Marx's ideas.*

1. Case in Point: Paul Lafargue

Take the example of Paul Lafargue, one of the founders of the Marxist (Guesdist) party in France and in his own mind a disciple of Marx. There is not much point in adding that he was also Marx's son-in-law since among his wedding gifts was *not* the gift of deep political and theoretical understanding. In *KMTR* 3, I have described Lafargue's "landmark" use of the term 'dictatorship of the proletariat' in 1888. To summarize it briefly:

Lafargue was, at this time, one of the people in the French Guesdist tendency who leaned toward critical support of the would-be military dictator General Boulanger. In fact, many saw Boulanger's movement as the "wave of the future." Like a whole section of the Blanquist group (which split), like a large number of independent leftists in the country, Lafargue wanted the movement to ride on the Boulangist nationalistic wave in order to be borne in to victory. These clever left-Boulangists might have said "After Boulanger we come!" like their future similars in Germany. Engels, in letters, strove to straighten Lafargue out, without success as long as the Man on Horseback was riding the popular wave.

Part of the left-Boulangist sentiment came from disgust with "parliamentarism," that is, with the ineffective and corrupt bourgeois-democratic institutions. Boulanger was going to rid France of "parliamentarist" paralysis and Get Things Done.

It was under these suspicious circumstances that Lafargue suddenly remembered that Marx himself had written something—somewhere—about "dictatorship." In an article "Parliamentarism and Boulangism," expounding his soft-on-Boulanger view, Lafargue inserted this remark:

When the proletariat . . . takes possession of the state, it will have to organize a revolutionary authority and rule society dictatorially until the bourgeoisie has disappeared as a class, i.e., until there has been completed the nationalization of the means of production . . .

There is no conception of *class* dictatorship here, and no reason to believe that Lafargue understood what it meant. Otherwise he would have known that "when the proletariat takes possession of the state" this already is the 'dictatorship of the proletariat.' Plainly Lafargue looked to the setting up of a special dictatorial authority outside democratic norms.

Lafargue was telling his Boulangist public: after all, we socialists want to "rule dictatorially" too . . .[1]

This was a notable harbinger of a pattern: grabbing at the phrase 'dictatorship of the proletariat' in order to advocate what Marx and Engels repudiated—and this even while Engels himself was still there to tug at Lafargue's sleeve and tell him that he was off the rails!

A materialist conception of *socialist* history should have no trouble understanding that (say) Lafargue, living and working in the French movement and in the crossroads of French politics, experienced Marx's ideas as only one peripheral influence on his own politics in the movement. Even Marx's ideas themselves, imperfectly grasped to begin with, were understood *within the framework* of traditional conceptions of the French movement which jostled inside Lafargue's skull along with what he had learned from Marx and tried to absorb with his characteristic superficiality.

We know from the Engels-Lafargue correspondence, fortunately, that Lafargue *did not "misunderstand" what Engels was telling him:* he rejected Engels' analysis. (No doubt he told himself that Engels "did not understand" Marx, who was safely dead.)

2. The "Misunderstanding"

If this cautionary view applied to some of the biggest questions of socialist politics, it must be kept in mind with redoubled attention when we come to the more difficult problem of the term 'dictatorship of the proletariat.' Here, as we have observed, "misunderstanding" became the rule. We have been able to find no case of a follower of Marx who really understood what Marx meant by the idea of "class dictatorship"—with one possible exception. And this remained true even after Engels' 1874 article (Locus 8), which explained the idea in apparently unmistakable terms.

Given that this happened so consistently, it can hardly be taken as simply a "misunderstanding." The people who "misunderstood" *wanted* to misunderstand: they already had a conception about 'dictatorship' which they had absorbed before they ever knew Marx, and they merely used—or ignored, or attacked—Marx's term in accordance with their own leanings.

The big "misunderstanding," already emphasized more than once in the preceding pages, concerned the view that 'dictatorship of the proletariat' referred to *specific governmental forms and policies*—"dictatorial" ones. Whereas for Marx and Engels the 'dictatorship of the proletariat' meant a workers' state, no more and no less, everyone else *assumed* that it referred to some special form of workers' state, a specially 'dictatorial' one. This assumption, too, was not merely the result of "misunderstanding": the very word 'dictatorship' was slowly changing its connotations in the course of the latter part of the nineteenth century, as we discussed in Chapter I. Every time Marx's phrase was picked up, it was less and less likely that the user even knew how elastic a term 'dictatorship' had been in the first half of the century. To this, add the following. The very motive for which Marx had invented the formulation in the first place—the confrontation with the Blanquist dictatorship—was now completely outlived. Marx's sense of the term no longer had its historical reason for existence.

There is a contrast that needs to be made clear. In not a single locus did Marx or Engels ever associate the use of the term 'dictatorship of the proletariat' with another question of obvious importance: the necessity for defending a victorious workers' state against counter-revolutionary force. They recognized this problem, of course; they discussed it—all socialists did—but they did not link it up as part of the definition of the 'dictatorship of the proletariat.' On the other hand, virtually every reference to 'dictatorship of the proletariat' made after their time was tied to *this* question explicitly or implicitly. The reason for this difference is plain enough: Marxist followers, asking themselves what the 'dictatorship' phrase meant, assumed that the answer could refer only to the task of suppressing counterrevolution after a conquest of political power.

In the socialist movement by the end of the century—as far as I know—*there was not one person using the word 'dictatorship' in any combination who showed awareness of the term's recent past,* who even suspected that Marx had used 'dictatorship' with a meaning no longer current.

There were naturally two types of reaction to this state of affairs: some rejected Marx's formulation because they rejected 'dictatorship'; some sought to find a justification for Marx's formulation by groping for a reinterpretation. These wound up as two different ways of burying Marx's thought.

In one way or another, the outcome is that, from this point on, we are no longer discussing Marx's, or Marx's and Engels', view of the 'dictatorship of the proletariat.' That view died with Engels. In its stead we will be dealing with a reinterpretation of the phrase which filled it with a special content.

This "misunderstanding" led directly to another one. If 'dictatorship of the proletariat' referred strictly to the class content of a *state,* the governmental form might vary widely, without affecting this class content. But if 'dictatorship' entailed specific governmental forms and policies (as it did in the "misunderstanding"), then it had to be implemented *by a particular government.* If we situate ourselves around the turn of the century, no socialist had any doubt that such a government, implementing the conquest of political power, had to be a government formed *by the revolutionary party,* the Social-Democratic Party. Conclusion, explicit or implicit: the 'dictatorship of the proletariat' could be exercised, or wielded, in practice only by the revolutionary party that had conquered power and instituted the revolutionary government.

For purposes of mental hygiene, the reader must dismiss the myth that the concept of the 'dictatorship of the party' was a devilish invention of "Leninism." We are going to investigate in Chapter 4 exactly what Lenin was responsible for, but he did not invent the concept that a 'dictatorship of the proletariat' had to be exercised in practice *through* the leadership ('dictatorship') of the party. Plekhanov had already thought this out, as Voden recounted. No one could say nay: once 'dictatorship of the proletariat' is understood to mean a particular 'dictatorial' government, what alternative can be even dreamed up? What else could be expected to stand at the head of a 'dictatorial' government?

Of course, a 'dictatorship of the proletariat' thus exercised via a 'dictatorship of the party' was taken to presage the introduction of complete democracy in government. We will eventually observe the point where the 'dictatorship of the party' concept turned into something else.

3. Eduard Bernstein

Bernstein's turn to "Revisionism" took place hard on Engels' death, and one (minor) point which Bernstein attacked involved the 'dictatorship of the proletariat.' Thenceforward it was inevitable that the term be entangled in the "Revisionist-Orthodox" controversy.

Bernstein's attack on the term, in his book *Evolutionary Socialism,* showed that he, who had worked closely with Engels for several years, had scarcely the vaguest notion of what it meant. To begin with, he recommended dropping the phrase on the ground that it was incompatible with parliamentary activity.

Is there any sense, for example, in maintaining the phrase of the "dictatorship of the proletariat" at a time when in all possible places representatives of Social-Democracy have placed themselves practically in the arena of Parliamentary work, have declared for the proportional representation of the people, and for direct legislation—all of which is inconsistent with dictatorship?

Bernstein pioneered the pattern (which we will meet again) of scornfully rejecting the very possibility that 'dictatorship' ever had a "weaker" meaning:

> The phrase [dictatorship of the proletariat] today is so antiquated that it is only to be reconciled with reality by stripping the word 'dictatorship' of its actual meaning and attaching to it some kind of weakened interpretation.

He then made what became his best-known comment on the term. Socialists, he argued, are "the pioneers of a higher civilization"—

> But the "dictatorship of the classes" belongs to a lower civilization, and apart from the question of the expediency and practicability of the thing, it is only to be looked upon as a reversion, as political atavism.[2]

This invented form "dictatorship of the classes" appears to be an attempt to reject the concept of a 'dictatorship of the bourgeoisie' along with the 'dictatorship of the proletariat': *any* idea of class dictatorship was the appurtenance of a "lower civilization." With this offhand dismissal he showed some awareness that Marx had spoken of a *class* dictatorship, but without the need to discuss the question politically.

4. *Wilhelm Liebknecht*

We have seen—in *KMTR 3*—that Liebknecht took part in the 1891 Reichstag discussion on the 'dictatorship of the proletariat,' but of course that performance was conditioned by the special exigencies of the situation.[3] In 1899, a year before his death, he wrote the essay entitled *No Compromise, No Election Deals* (more properly: No Election Alliance) which became one of his best-known productions. It should not be supposed that he really rejected all "compromise" and every "election alliance": the title was one of his revolutionary poses.

However, we are concerned here with the passage on the 'dictatorship of the proletariat.'

Liebknecht repudiated this term without so much as mentioning Marx's name. This enabled him to start off by charging that the whole thing was the invention of the bourgeois politicians (really!):

> The innumerable sins and vices which they attribute to us contain not a single one which has not originated in their own minds.
>
> To add one new example to the old list, I would like to mention merely the allegation, which has become a stock phrase in the last twenty years, that the aim of Social-Democracy is *the dictatorship of the proletariat*.

It is difficult to say what he may have had in mind by his reference to the "last twenty years": if 'dictatorship of the proletariat' became a "stock phrase," even in Germany, this development has escaped notice. It is simpler to assume he did not know what he was talking about.

Liebknecht then swung into the same *tu quoque* tactic as in his 1891 speech, by a denunciation of the "dictatorship of the bourgeoisie":

> The truth is that ever *since the June battle in Paris,* that is for fifty-one years, we have in fact had the *dictatorship of the bourgeoisie* on the European continent. A dictatorship which has used fire and sword against the working class; which brought us the horrible bloodbath of the Commune after the battle of June, and hundreds of smaller massacres of workers; a dictatorship which *deprives* the working class of its civil rights and debars the proletariat not only from the enjoyment of political rights, but also from elementary legal rights; a dictatorship which has enacted dozens of exceptional laws, gag laws, and which we Germans have to thank for the Anti-Socialist Law, the penal servitude policy and numerous sentences based on class legislation . . .[4]

He wound up with a repudiation in so many words:

> Not the establishment of a dictatorship of the proletariat, but *the destruction of the dictatorship of the bourgeoisie* is the object of the political power which Social-Democracy wants to attain . . .[5]

Since Liebknecht did not mention Marx's name but spoke only of the party, his last statement was technically correct: the "Social-Democracy" had, in fact, virtually repudiated Marx in 1891. Lenin, writing a laudatory preface in December 1906 for a Russian translation of Liebknecht's pamphlet, made no reference whatever to this passage, as he used Liebknecht to cudgel the Mensheviks.[6]

5. Jean Jaurès

A year after Liebknecht's death, *Vorwärts* for August 7, 1901, published an unfinished meditation of his on the future society, from his posthumous papers, discussing "how socialism will be realized." In Paris Jaurès read it, chortled, and proceeded to write a series of articles with extensive quotations from Liebknecht's manuscript, showing that in essence the "Soldier of the Revolution" agreed with Bernstein's parliamentary, legalistic, peaceful road to office, despite the former's revolutionary reputation. The articles were included in Jaurès' *Etudes Socialistes* in 1902. To introduce this collection Jaurès wrote an essay, "Question de Méthode," addressed to Charles Péguy.* This introduction to the book turned out to be—a polemic against the 'dictatorship of the proletariat.'

Engels' "Critique of the Erfurt Program" (with Locus 12) had been published in the *Neue Zeit* in 1901; perhaps this had stimulated Jaurès to adopt the 'dictatorship of the proletariat' as his tackling-dummy. However, in this introduction Jaurès made no reference to any statement about the 'dictatorship of the proletariat' actually made by Marx or Engels; his only specific reference was to the phrase 'impersonal dictatorship of the proletariat,' which was Vaillant's hallmark. In fact—difficult though it is to credit—Jaurès referred almost only to the *Communist Manifesto* and repeatedly wrote as if the Manifesto called for a 'dictatorship of the proletariat.'

The political content of Jaurès' book was fullblooded parliamentary reformism in the French manner (i.e., with verbal bows to the French revolutionary tradition). His method was to link every revolutionary idea with dictatorship, and reject it as such in the name of 'democracy,' which he defined in the same generalized and nonclass legal forms as Bernstein.

According to the Manifesto, said Jaurès, the proletariat "conquers

---

*This Charles Péguy, it happens, is quoted in Wolfe's *Three Who Made a Revolution* as asking in 1900: "I should like to know who will actually be the persons who will exercise the dictatorship of the proletariat . . ."[7] Leaving aside Wolfe's evident belief that this probes to the heart of the matter, it must be observed that Péguy is not an impressive example of a democrat. As the *Encyclopaedia of the Social Sciences* noted, "In many respects Péguy anticipated the philosophy of fascism."[8] He broke with socialism at just about the time that Jaurès was dedicating his anti-Marx polemic to him, and started on his road to a mystic nationalist-chauvinist Catholicism.

democracy" (quoting the well-known passage near the end of Section II)—

> that is, in fact it suspends democracy, since it substitutes the dictatorial will of a class for the will of the majority of the citizens freely consulted. It is by force, by dictatorial power, that it commits these first "despotic inroads" on property that the Manifesto foresees.[9]

In case the reader missed it: Jaurès here assumed, through the power of mistranslation, that the Manifesto's famous statement about "winning democracy" means *suspending* democracy! He proceeded to wonder whether Marx and Engels "dreamed of suspending democracy for a long time, for the benefit of the proletarian dictatorship." For several paragraphs he continued thus simply counterposing Marx's "dictatorship," understood in the crudest dictatorial sense, to ordinary "democracy," which he described in purely bourgeois-democratic terms. He also echoed Bernstein's point about "atavism":

> But those socialists today who still speak of the "impersonal dictatorship of the proletariat" or who look to the brusque taking of power and to violence done to democracy, these retrogress to the time when the proletariat was still weak and reduced to artificial methods of winning.[10]

Obviously he assumed, with no necessity of investigation, that Marx had in mind simply a minority putsch, and indeed he lumped Marx and Blanqui together in arguing that the "method of revolution" is dead in the present civilized world. "The passage to complete democracy will be accomplished without a revolutionary crisis."[11]

All this was a statement of the standpoint of the social-democratic reform wing in full flower: only, in this case Jaurès chose to hang the exposition on his belief that the *Communist Manifesto* had advocated a class dictatorship, a dictatorship of the proletariat.

6. Karl Liebknecht and Others

The German edition of Jaurès' book, *Aus Theorie und Praxis*, translated by Südekum, was published in 1902 by the press of the Bernsteinian organ *Sozialistische Monatshefte*. In the *Neue Zeit*, Wilhelm Liebknecht's son Karl, then 31, wrote a review, "Die neue Methode," on the "question of method" which had been the theme of

Jaurès' introduction. As a preliminary to this discussion, Karl Liebknecht detailed some of Jaurès' misunderstandings of Marxism, especially in respect to the *Communist Manifesto,* which (as he says with justice) Jaurès used "almost exclusively." One point interests us:

Also on the dictatorship of the proletariat and the program of revolution Jaurès falls into a crucial error. As mentioned, the Manifesto presupposes a victory by the *majority* of the people, whose rule is certainly consistent with democracy. But just because a class *rule* of the proletariat (though democratic) should be stabilized and this class rule should be applied to an energetic utilization of the state machinery in the proletarian sense, the Manifesto speaks of the "dictatorship" of the proletariat. This is—as Engels' programmatic letter [on the Erfurt Program] also shows—the sense especially of the statements on page 24 of the Manifesto [about "winning democracy"] . . .[12]

It is again hard to believe, but Karl Liebknecht assumed—along with Jaurès—that "the Manifesto speaks of the 'dictatorship' of the proletariat." Clearly, none of these people knew very much about what Marx had written, even in the Manifesto.

Karl L. did make the valid point that Marx assumed a majority-based regime. Why then a 'dictatorship'? The answer here seemed to say, rather vaguely, that a dictatorship was needed to "stabilize" (meaning "defend"?) the rule of the proletariat, and to ensure "an energetic utilization of the state machinery." This effort was no worse than others we will see.

Before closing this chapter with two of the major figures in our story, let us throw in some minor cases. There is no plethora of instances to choose from; but here are three.

(1) Charles Longuet, Marx's rightwingish son-in-law, wrote a preface to a French edition of Marx's *Civil War in France* in 1900. He had this to say on our subject:

. . . it is not to be doubted that the historical event of 1871 [the Commune] gave its true meaning to the ambiguous formula of 1847 [sic], which was too simplistic in any case: dictatorship of the proletariat. No Marxist worthy of the name has the right today—nor the intention, I think—to attribute to the authors of the *Communist Manifesto* the idea of substituting the despotism of the working class for the domination of the capitalist class . . .[13]

Like Jaurès and Karl Liebknecht, Longuet was apparently convinced that the "ambiguous formula" had appeared in the Manifesto (hence his date "1847," a common error for the Manifesto's publication year). In any case, he did not undertake to explain why the 'dictatorship of the proletariat' was not equivalent to the 'despotism of the working class.' He would much prefer to forget the whole thing. (Even the expression "civil war" in the title of Marx's work made him uneasy: he changed Marx's title to *The Paris Commune*.)

(2) In Germany, Werner Sombart's *Socialism and the Social Movement* (first edition published in 1896) had something to say on our subject. We have elsewhere mentioned[14] his philistine observation about "that crazy notion, worthy only of a Blanqui, of the dictatorship of the proletariat." According to him, Marx's view of the dictatorship of the proletariat

> sets forth that the change from the capitalist to the socialist system of society will be brought about by an act of violence. The proletariat will seize political power and carry through a scheme of legislation which shall establish the new order.

Marx believed that

> the new order is ready-made and complete (i.e., in the minds of so-cialists), and all that is necessary is to take steps to get it established. Only when we imagine a view like this to have been in the mind of Marx can we understand his position at the time of the rising of the Commune in 1871—the maddest of all risings, which had not the least chance of success.[15]

To top this, Sombart insisted here—more than once—that "the idea of the dictatorship of the proletariat may be traced to Robespierre."

There is something about the 'dictatorship of the proletariat' that brings out the worst in commentators: Sombart did not usually do this fuddled-philistine bit.

(3) And now to something a bit better. Charles Vérecque's *Dictionnaire du Socialisme* (1911) is very uneven, but its entry on "Dictature du prolétariat" was not the worst version written in those years. It even quoted the Marx locus from the "Critique of the Gotha Program" (only omitting the word 'revolutionary,' to be sure) and ended with a long citation from Charles Bonnier's article of 1897. It had this to say on the term:

> The proletariat will take and maintain possession of the state only for the time necessary for humanity to regain possession of the social wealth.

The period during which it will wield [state power] will constitute the dictatorship of the proletariat. [Marx is then quoted . . .] When Engels was asked what he understood by dictatorship of the proletariat, he replied by pointing to the Paris Commune. Exactly so. Tomorrow, as in 1871 but in other circumstances and with other aims, the proletarians will take hold of the state and use it to construct the new society. And so long as they have not yet completed their mission, they will naturally be in a condition of dictatorship [*en état de dictature*]. This dictatorship will be longer or shorter depending on the economic development of society and on whether the bourgeoisie will leave the new order of things alone or seek to oppose it.[16]

Bonnier's important contribution is presented in Special Note A.

7. Karl Kautsky

Looking ahead to the Lenin-Kautsky controversy of 1919–1920, it will be especially interesting to see what Kautsky wrote about the 'dictatorship of the proletariat' during the Second International period when he was regarded as the theoretical "pope" of Marxism. The picture to be presented is a very muddled one.

There were four writings in which the term came from his pen before 1917.

(1) Kautsky's initial discussion came in the midst of another and different muddle. It started in 1893 when Franz Mehring wrote in the *Neue Zeit,* in a leftist mood:

The outlook which has it that once the majority of a bourgeois parliament consists of class-conscious workers the road is open to the socialist society—this outlook is like a knife that lacks both handle and blade. Only when the faith of the masses in bourgeois parliamentarism is entirely dead does the road to the future open up.

In a brochure on *Parliamentarism, Popular Legislation and the Social-Democracy* which was known to be directed against Mehring's view, Kautsky wrote as follows:

Only one who is politically blind can still maintain today that the representative system even under the sway of universal suffrage ensures the rule of the bourgeoisie, and that in order to overthrow the latter one must first get rid of the representative system. Now it is already beginning to become obvious that a truly parliamentary system can be just as good an instrument of the dictatorship of the proletariat as it is an instrument of the dictatorship of the bourgeoisie.

In letters written at this time to Mehring, Kautsky averred that for the dictatorship of the proletariat he could think of no other form than an energetic parliament after the English model with a Social-Democratic majority; it even remained to be seen if the English model could constitute the basis for the proletarian dictatorship if it retained its monarchical head.[17]

The first confusion here was over 'parliamentarism.' Kautsky's reply made 'parliamentarism' equivalent to 'representative system,' which he defended as if it could be realized only in the existing bourgeois forms. Whatever Mehring meant by 'parliamentarism,' it is unlikely that he was advocating the elimination of all representative systems.

Into this muddle, Kautsky's brochure injected another question, indubitably important—so important that it deserved to be handled only with the greatest clarity. He could not have been "politically blind" to the fact that he was broaching a problem on which Marx had made himself quite clear, precisely in connection with parliamentarism. We have to disentangle these ideas in order to see how the 'dictatorship of the proletariat' figures in them.

The Commune state was based on a representative system. Marx's *Civil War in France,* as we have seen, had gone into great and laudatory detail on the representative-democratic features of the Commune form—features that made it essentially *more* democratic than bourgeois parliaments. At the same time Marx had treated this state form as one distinct from and opposed to a "parliamentary" system. "The Commune," said the Address, "was to be a working, not a parliamentary, body, executive and legislative at the same time."[18] In other passages too, there could be no doubt that, at least in Marx's vocabulary, the parliamentary system was *one* type of representative system, a bourgeois type which he counterposed to the Commune state.

The Civil War in France had had another thing to say about the parliamentary state machine: "the working class cannot simply lay hold of the ready-made state machinery, and wield it for its own purposes."[19] Marx had considered this lesson of experience so important that it had been prominently repeated as the main political amendment to be made to the *Communist Manifesto*.[20]

Now what Kautsky was doing was proposing to wield the ready-made parliamentary-state machinery for socialist purposes. Contrary to the implications of later polemics, this proposal was not *ipso facto* anti-Marx, especially in respect to England: it is well known that Marx had more than once suggested the *possibility* that a socialist conquest of power might be inaugurated in England and some other countries with the winning of a parliamentary majority. What would happen *after* such an inauguration might be another matter; as Engels had emphasized on this point, Marx "certainly never forgot to add that he hardly expected the English ruling classes to submit, without a 'proslavery rebellion,' to this peaceful and legal revolution."[21]

This reminder, which Marx had made himself before Engels repeated it, implied that the winning of a parliamentary majority by peaceful-legal means only constituted the *first* act in a socialist revolution, after which the state power thus established under the dominion of the proletariat would be obliged to confirm its own power in the extraparliamentary field. How an embattled workers' state might have to change, or adapt, the "ready-made" forms was entirely open to discussion and experience; likewise, how a workers' state that was at last secure might alter the state machinery preparatory to its withering away.

These issues were open to reasonable discussion among Marxists as well as with other socialists; but Kautsky's presentation did not treat the question within this framework. His treatment had the force of insisting on the parliamentary form of the 'dictatorship of the proletariat' as dogmatically as the principled "antiparliamentarians" of the anarchosyndicalist school did in their own simplistic way. (Historically, social-democratic parliamentarism has been the opposite side of the same coin as the anarchoid forms of antiparliamentarism.) Where Marx and Engels had viewed the "peaceful and legal" route as a limited possibility for very few countries under special conditions, Kautsky seemed to be proposing something like it as the general rule—hence in the first place *for Germany*, where the Reichstag was still only the "figleaf of absolutism."

Now this whole issue (the role of force in revolution versus the peaceful-legal road to power) is not our subject here; and not only can we not continue it, we must wonder why Kautsky injected the 'dictatorship of the proletariat' into it in the first place. Of course, the movement had not forgotten how Engels' talk of the 'dictatorship of the proletariat' had rocked it only two years before—a rumpus which had made the term a symbol of revolutionary leanings. I have a suspicion: that precisely because the main point Kautsky was making sounded like a concession to reformism, he dressed it in the timely "revolutionary" garb of the 'dictatorship of the proletariat.'

The outcome was that in this use of 'dictatorship of the proletariat' Kautsky simply seemed to mean a workers' state, nothing more and nothing less: a rare case. This result may well have been fortuitous, unintentional: he may have meant that a parliamentary state could carry out 'dictatorial' measures as well as any other; and to be sure, the bourgeois parliamentary state had shown how dictatorial it could get.

(2) Kautsky's next use of the term came in 1895, in the first volume of an ambitious (and unfinished) collective enterprise, a multivolume history of socialism. This volume dealt with *The Forerunners of Modern Socialism.*[22] The passage came in Part 3 ("Communism in the Middle Ages and in the Age of the Reformation") of an essay called *From Plato to the Anabaptists.* Writing of the communism of the heretical sects, he contrasted the medieval movements (Münzer's in the forefront) with the communism of the early Christians:

> Early Christian communism was not political and not activist. In contrast, proletarian communism, from the Middle Ages on, has had, as a matter of natural necessity, the tendency to become political and rebellious, given favorable circumstances. Like the present-day Social-Democracy, it set itself the aim of the *dictatorship of the proletariat* as the most effective lever for bringing about the communist society.[23]

This is a surprising place for the term to pop up! To think of a dictatorship of the proletariat by (say) the Taborites or the Bohemian Brethren, or even Münzer's movement, takes some stretching of the imagination. I cannot avoid the suspicion, again, that the term was dragged in.

(3) Then came the Bernsteiniad; and, as mentioned, Bernstein's book made the 'dictatorship of the proletariat' a target of attack. Kautsky's reply, *Bernstein and the Social-Democratic Program,* took up the gage in 1899.

Now the "misunderstanding" of the term's meaning became as plain in the defender as in the attacker. "Bernstein indignantly rejects the idea of a dictatorship of the proletariat," Kautsky wrote, but it is not true that the contradictions of this society are becoming milder . . .

On the contrary! I wouldn't swear that the class rule of the proletariat must take on the forms of a class dictatorship. But experience up to now and expectations for the future do not at all prove that democratic forms are sufficient to make the class rule of the proletariat superfluous to its emancipation.[24]

Here, if not before, it was unmistakably clear that the "class rule of the proletariat" might or might not entail "class dictatorship"; that is, "dictatorship" meant special dictatorial measures, something outside "democratic forms." And by the latter term, remember, Kautsky meant *parliamentary* forms. He did not want to decide in advance what the special *un*democratic measures might be:

> We can calmly leave to the future the decision on the problem of proletarian dictatorship. On this too we do not need to tie our hands.[25]

He had one other reference to 'dictatorship,' plainly used somewhat differently:

> When [the capitalists] today complain about the terrorism of the proletariat, this is silly phrasemongering. However, dictatorship in the factory will necessarily devolve upon the proletariat once it has achieved mastery in the state.[26]

By "dictatorship in the factory" he seems to have meant that the proletariat would do away with the capitalist mode of production, thus making a "social revolution."[27] It would be digressive to follow his further discussion of the role of force and the definition of the word 'revolution.'

(4) The zenith of Kautsky's prewar leftism came in 1909 with the publication of his brochure *The Road to Power*. Its first chapter, on "The Conquest of Political Power," maintained that it was becoming "clearer and clearer that a revolution is still possible only as a *proletarian* revolution," and "when once the proletariat is the only revolutionary class in the nation," then "the sole regime that can replace the existing one is a *proletarian* regime."[28] On the other hand, there were socialists who thought to do without a revolution by entering a coalition government with bourgeois parties. The Bernsteinians argued that by coalitionism socialists utilized the antagonisms among different sections of the ruling class, and recognized that there was not one "reactionary mass." Yes, Kautsky replied—Marx and Engels were eager to utilize the differences among bourgeois and they opposed the "reactionary mass" concept, but—

However much Marx and Engels were in favor of using the differences among bourgeois parties to further proletarian aims, however much they opposed the phrase "reactionary mass," nonetheless they coined the phrase *dictatorship of the proletariat,*★ which Engels still championed in 1891 shortly before his death—this phrase expressing the proletariat's sole dominion as the only form in which it can exercise political power.[30]

This statement is interesting in that it seems to revert to treating 'dictatorship of the proletariat' as simply a synonym for 'workers' state.' Had Kautsky abandoned his view about 'parliamentarism'? There is no evidence that he did. Was he conscious of the difference implied in the conception of the 'dictatorship of the proletariat' between this statement and the one in 1899? Unlikely.

When we ask whether the prewar Kautsky made a distinction, like everyone else, between a workers' state and a dictatorship of the proletariat, if we try to figure out whether he defined the latter term with special dictatorial attributes, we would have to reply along these lines: since apparently he was not even conscious of the question, how can we deduce a sure answer from formulations that might well have been happenstantial? In my opinion, what was still muddling the issue, *inter alia,* was Kautsky's tendency to equate 'representative democracy' with one of its forms, 'parliamentarism.'

The reply is not satisfactory, to be sure, but it reflects the confused situation. In any case we should keep it in mind when we come to the peculiar stance he took in 1918.

8. Rosa Luxemburg

It is appropriate to end this chapter with a figure who represented a Polish bridge between the Western European movement, particularly the German movement, and the Russians of the next chapter.

More important: as far as I have been able to determine, Rosa Luxemburg consistently and without exception used the term 'dic-

---

★When A. M. Simons, a leading American socialist editor and *soi-disant* Marxist, translated Kautsky's brochure (the same year, 1909), his rendering of *Diktatur des Proletariats* was "dictation of the proletariat."[29] The phrase could not have been very familiar to the American socialist public.

tatorship of the proletariat' in the manner of Marx and Engels—the only one to do so consistently in our entire account. That is, she used 'dictatorship of the proletariat' to mean a workers' state with *no* implication that it necessarily entailed special dictatorial measures or attributes without which it could not be called a 'dictatorship.'

At any rate, so I interpret the passages in her writings, which will now be laid before the reader. The case is such that one must keep thinking of what is *not* in the passage, what she is not saying about 'dictatorship of the proletariat.'

(1) Luxemburg's brochure *Social Reform or Revolution?* was published in 1899 as her main reply to Bernstein's Revisionism. She did not refer directly to Bernstein's remarks on 'dictatorship of the proletariat.' The issue entered into her discussion as she took up the movement's attitude to democracy. Bernstein had invoked Marx's approval of a possible buy-out of the landlords. Certainly, Luxemburg replied: but Marx was naturally assuming that the proletariat had *already* conquered political power when this question came up—

> For obviously a "buy-out" of the ruling classes can come up only when the working class is at the helm. What Marx therefore took into consideration here as a possibility is the *peaceful exercise of the proletarian dictatorship* and not the substitution of capitalist social reforms for dictatorship.[31]

This statement stands out in the literature we have surveyed, since the general assumption was that the 'dictatorship' aspect of the 'dictatorship of the proletariat' meant precisely its organization of force to suppress bourgeois elements. But the "buy-out" was a case (however unusual) of a *noncoercive* exercise of workers' power. This *noncoercive* measure was here called the "peaceful exercise" of the dictatorship of the proletariat, that is, of workers' power.

(2) In the course of an article published in early 1903 about the development of the Polish movement, Luxemburg summarized the Marxist conception of the relationship of immediate socialist tasks to final goals. Central to this explanation was the following passage:

> Starting out from the principle of scientific socialism that "the emancipation of the working class can only be the work of the working class itself," the Social-Democracy recognizes that the overthrow, that is, the revolution to realize the socialist reorganization, can only be carried through by the working class as such, indeed the really broad *mass* of the

workers, above all the mass of the industrial proletariat. The first act of the socialist transformation must therefore be the conquest of political power *by the working class* and the establishment of the *dictatorship of the proletariat,* which is absolutely necessary for effecting transitional measures.[32]

We see that "conquest of political power" and "dictatorship of the proletariat" are treated as virtually the same act.

(3) The Revolution of 1905 rocked all European socialists, but the Polish Marxists were at the center of the hurricane along with the Russians. In early 1906 Luxemburg published a brochure entitled *1649—1789—1905* on the problems of the revolution; the term 'dictatorship of the proletariat' came up three times in a couple of pages. First:

> The proletariat in Russia . . . carries on the struggle against both absolutism and capitalism. It only wants the forms of bourgeois democracy, but it wants them *for itself,* for the purposes of the proletarian class struggle. It wants the *eight-hour day,* the people's militia, the republic— demands that simply point to bourgeois society, not socialist. But these demands at the same time press so hard on the outermost *borders* of the rule of capital that they appear as transitional forms to a proletarian dictatorship.[33]

The Russian revolution that is going on, she said, has a new weapon, the revolutionary mass strike, and is a new type of revolution:

> In form bourgeois-democratic, in essence proletarian-socialist, it is by both content and methods a *transitional form* from the bourgeois revolution of the past to the proletarian revolution of the future, in which the dictatorship of the proletariat and the realization of socialism are already involved.

The same paragraph concludes that these stormy events "can have no other outcome than the social revolution—the dictatorship of the proletariat."[34]

(4) Shortly thereafter, the same year, Luxemburg wrote a commentary on the program of her Polish party, published as a pamphlet in both Polish and German, titled *What Do We Want?* In a concise summary of the views of revolutionary Marxism, Section II dealt with the state and revolution:

> In short: as introduction to the realization of socialism, it is necessary that for a certain period the working class exercise sole power [*Alleinherr-*

schaft] in the state, that is, that it *establish the dictatorship of the working class.*[35]

And a little farther on:

> For the realization of socialism it is necessary for the proletariat to seize state power and use it with a strong hand to uproot present-day social institutions. But the dictatorship of the proletariat will be, generally speaking, the *last* case of the employment of force in the history of mankind and the first case of its employment on behalf of the broad masses of the disinherited.[36]

The end of the pamphlet summarized the goals:

> . . . toward the conquest of political power in the state, toward the introduction of the dictatorship of the proletariat, and toward the realization of socialism.[37]

(5) Still in 1906, Luxemburg published one of her most important brochures, on *Mass Strike, Party and Trade Unions.* Its seventh chapter argued that there could no longer be talk of a bourgeois revolution in Germany:

> And therefore, in a period of open political struggles by the people in Germany, it can only be a question now of the *dictatorship of the proletariat* as the historically necessary final goal.[38]

(6) By 1910, when the revolutionary impact of 1905 had died down, the German Revisionist wing plucked up courage to act out its views while thumbing a collective nose at party discipline. In July the Social-Democratic deputies in the Baden legislature voted in their majority in favor of the government's budget; the party congress would condemn this action in September. In a long article in the *Neue Zeit* on "Theory and Practice," Luxemburg tied the "party crisis" up with other issues, and took occasion to polemize against Kautsky's rejection of the mass strike as a revolutionary weapon.

In the course of this article Luxemburg quoted Engels' passage (Locus 12) in the "Critique of the Erfurt Program"; but what she was interested in, at this point, was the demand for a democratic republic.[39] Further along, she spoke of the proletariat "struggling for its dictatorship," using this expression simply as a synonym for its conquest of power.[40]

(7) In August 1917—that is, on the eve of the Bolshevik seizure of power in Russia—Luxemburg, now a leader of the revolutionary

Spartacus group in Germany, published a substantial analysis of the current situation of the revolution in Russia: "Burning Questions of the Day," in *Spartacus,* No. 6. Of its four sections, the second was titled "The Dictatorship of the Proletariat."

It should be noted that Luxemburg was involved, like the Russian Social-Democrats of the various factions, in the disputes over "democratic dictatorship of the proletariat and the peasantry" versus "dictatorship of the proletariat," etc. Her employment of 'dictatorship of the proletariat' in such discussions must be seen in the Russian context, rather than in reference to preceding disputes in the German movement. Her position was based on the viewpoint (roughly similar to Trotsky's) that the coming revolution in Russia would *have* to take directly socialist measures, unlike Lenin's conceptual "democratic [i.e., bourgeois-democratic] dictatorship," which was restricted to bourgeois-democratic tasks.★

This accounts for the prominence of the term in this 1917 article. In regard to the class struggle in Russian society, she emphasized that "the goal toward which development is steering is inevitably the dictatorship of the socialist proletariat." One wonders whether, in the heat of a moment when the issues were far from merely theoretical, she was conscious of what this apparently slight variation meant: "dictatorship of the *socialist* proletariat"? Over nonsocialist proletarians? The answer could be, of course, that since the proletariat was prosocialist in its majority, the adjective "socialist" was not a restrictive modifier but simply descriptive.

In the next paragraph:

> The new coalition cabinet, by virtue of the inner logical development, sooner or later will have to give way to a purely socialist government, i.e., to the actual and formal dictatorship of the proletariat. Here, however, the destiny of the Russian revolution begins. The dictatorship of the proletariat in Russia—supposing that an international proletarian revolution does not come to its support in good time—is doomed to a stunning defeat, in comparison with which the fate of the Paris Commune would be child's play. [41]

She continued to use the term as a synonym for the proletarian conquest of power:

★This anticipates the discussion in the next chapter on the differences among the Russian factions (Bolsheviks, Mensheviks, Trotsky); see Chapter 3, Section 4.

The closer the dictatorship of the proletariat approaches in Russia, the more there matures the inevitable reversion of the Russian bourgeoisie back into the arms of the counterrevolution. . . .

Finally, however, the closer the dictatorship of the proletariat draws near in Russia, the more the crusade of the whole European bourgeoisie against the Russian republic gets set.[42]

We will come back to Luxemburg's post-1917 views. Looking over the seven specimens above, we have to confirm the initial observation: in not one of these passages did she make the assumption that virtually everyone else did—that 'dictatorship of the proletariat' had a special dictatorial meaning related to the problem of suppressing counter-revolution by force. It goes without saying that she was perfectly aware of the latter need, and discussed it freely as a voice of the revolutionary wing of the movement. *But she did not discuss it under the rubric of the 'dictatorship of the proletariat'*—this was her distinction.

3
Plekhanov
and Other Russians

Sidney Hook has written in his *Marx and the Marxists:*

> As Marxism as a movement developed, the phrase "dictatorship of the proletariat" fell into almost total disuse in every politically democratic country until it was revived by the followers of Lenin and Trotsky.[1]

This is the myth: every part of Hook's statement is a falsifiction. If we limit ourselves to politically democratic countries, hence exclude Russia, then the phrase was never in general use by any socialist party or section of the movement, and so it could not have fallen into disuse. If we include Russia, as Hook does in his last clause, then it was not Lenin or Trotsky or their followers who revived it. Furthermore, Hook's coupling of the two names makes sense only if he is referring to the post-1917 period—but the term had been "revived," or at least vivified, at the beginning of the century, when the Russian Social-Democratic Labor Party itself was organized.

Devotees of the devil-theory of Leninism will be surprised to learn that the man responsible was no Bolshevik but the "Father of Russian Marxism," Georgi V. Plekhanov.

And what Plekhanov "revived" was not Marx's view but a fateful substitute.

1. Plekhanov's 'Dictatorship'

We have already seen that Engels learned of Plekhanov's view of the 'dictatorship of the proletariat' in 1893, and commented that the application of this view would wreck the movement.[2] While Plekhanov was never faced with the problem of actually establishing a dictatorship of the proletariat, he did get a chance to do something a little less sweeping: he established it in the program of the Russian party.

During the period of the Second International, Plekhanov stood out as a party leader who kept mentioning the 'dictatorship of the proletariat' favorably from time to time, even before Engels' death. It would be hard to explain this if it had meant to him what it had meant to Marx; obviously it meant something else—as we know anyway. It was associated in his mind with special dictatorial measures of suppression, the need for which had appeared to him even before he ever heard of Marx's term. In his case as in others', the term became a peg on which to hang this line of thought.

Plekhanov was much more cautious in his public statements than in the private views he expressed to comrades like Voden. Ten years before Voden's talk with Engels, Plekhanov had written about the 'dictatorship of the proletariat' in his very first work of Marxist inspiration, a pamphlet called *Socialism and the Political Struggle*. Since he himself was developing out of left-wing Narodism, his polemic was turned in that direction: we need the seizure of political power by a revolutionary party . . . a revolutionary class in power will defend itself against reaction with "the mighty weapon of state power" . . . but there is a world of difference between "the dictatorship of a class" and the dictatorship of a group of revolutionary intelligentsia: "This applies in particular to the dictatorship of the working class. . . ." He emphasized that it had to be carried out by the workers themselves and not under tutelage.[3] Indeed, the emphasis here on *class* dictatorship was unusual—especially for the year 1883.

Two years later, Plekhanov's more important work *Our Differences* offered a passage of the greatest interest. It had two parts: first it presented the views of Peter Lavrov, an influential leader of revolutionary Narodism who had long been a friend and correspondent of Marx and Engels, though not a Marxist; and then Plekhanov commented on these views.

Lavrov, in an 1874 brochure, was attacking the standard Narodnik idea of revolution and dictatorship: "a revolution carried out by a minority, with a more or less lasting dictatorship of that minority"—the "Jacobin dictatorship" (what Western historians would semi-automatically call 'Blanquism').★ Lavrov's polemic against this "theory of the revolutionary dictatorship of a minority" was based on the following argument, which deserves a little space:

> History has shown [wrote Lavrov], and psychology convinces us, that any unlimited power, any dictatorship, spoils even the best people and that even men of genius who wished to confer blessings on the people by means of decrees could not do so. Every dictatorship must surround itself with coercive force, blindly obedient tools; every dictatorship has had to suppress by force not only reactionaries, but also people who simply did not agree with its methods; every dictatorship seized by force has had to spend more time, efforts and energy fighting its rivals for power than carrying out its program by means of that power. *But dreams of the termination of a dictatorship seized violently by any party can be entertained only before the seizure;* in the parties' struggle for power, in the agitation of overt and covert intrigues, every minute brings new necessity for maintaining power and reveals new impossibility of abandoning it. The dictatorship can be wrenched from the hands of the dictators only by a new revolution. . . .
>
> Does our revolutionary youth indeed agree to be the base of the throne of a few dictators who, even *with most selfless intentions, can be only new sources of social calamities,* and who, most probably, will not even be selfless fanatics, but men of passionate ambition thirsting for power for power's sake, craving for power for themselves? . . .[4]

Lavrov continued by averring that his own tendency, "the party of the popular social revolution," would fight against this Russian Jacobinism, "directly one of them reaches out for power."

Having done the service of quoting all this, Plekhanov then took the floor back: he agreed with Lavrov's opinion, he stated, but had "arrived at our conviction by a somewhat different path." Typically, he objected to Lavrov's approach as "subjective," because it was concerned with "the thoughts and feelings of individual personalities— even if they had the title of dictator."★★ He wanted to put the spotlight on the "objective side," "the social conditions."

★Lavrov's target was the Blanquist-style Narodnik Peter Tkachev, who had recently been his collaborator. Tkachev wanted a conspiratorial elite that would seize power, "subservient to one common leadership," to establish a "collective dictatorship." As for the axiom that "power corrupts," he stood it on its head: it would be no factor whatsoever with *his* "selfless dictators," he claimed.[5] To be sure, Tkachev was an extreme case. For Engels' polemic against him, see his "Social Questions in Russia."[6]

★★What was typical of Plekhanov's approach was his flat counterposition of "subjective" and "objective," simply rejecting the former; he no doubt considered this to be an

. . . we think that if "the emancipation of the workers must be conquered by the workers themselves," there is nothing any dictatorship can
do when the working class "in town and country" has not been prepared
for the socialist revolution. And that preparation generally proceeds
parallel to the development of the productive forces and of the organization of production corresponding to them.[7]

His argument seemed to point to the conclusion that a *premature*
dictatorship could not accomplish the "social and political miracles"
expected. As for Lavrov's fear that "any dictatorship spoils even the
best people," he demurred.

The main outcome of his argumentation was that a minority dictatorship could not achieve socialism (his area of agreement with
Lavrov), but his general rejection of Lavrov's *case* against minority
dictatorship left a great deal up in the air—even about the use of
dictatorial measures by a revolution conceived to be based on a
majority.

In 1892 and 1893 Plekhanov's passing references to the 'dictatorship
of the proletariat' were uninformative, but one must pause at the fact
that his short article of 1893, in the French party's organ, ended with
an italicized invocation of *"the dictatorship of the proletariat as a means to
attain the end which is the socialist organization of production":* that is, he
used the term virtually as a routine agitational synonym for the
socialist goal in general.[8] This sort of thing will not be commonly
seen in the socialist press until after 1917.

With the turn of the century Plekhanov's further references to the
term concerned Bernstein's attack on it. This led to an especially long
passage in his introduction to a new edition of the *Communist Manifesto*
published in 1900. As before, he defined the 'dictatorship of the
proletariat' in terms of suppression:

As we have pointed out, the dictatorship of any class means its supremacy, which permits it to dispose of the organized force of society to

---

application of the materialist conception of history. It is a false dichotomy: the "subjective" (that is, politico-psychological) consequences of dictatorship, or any other sociopolitical phenomenon, are closely linked with *and a part of* the total social situation—
what Plekhanov calls "the objective side of the matter." Lavrov's approach would be
incompatible with Marx's only if the former rejected or neglected this link, as he did
not. Plekhanov, among other things, was a pioneer of that muscle-bound "Marxism"
which tended to convince people that historical materialism was a one-sided formula
that could not encompass the interaction between political psychology and other social
factors.

defend its interests and suppress all social movements that directly or indirectly threaten those interests.[9]

At this point, it must be said, his discussion of the idea was in terms of *class* dictatorship, bourgeois or proletarian.[10]

All this was merely preliminary to the main show in 1903.

2. 'Dictatorship' at the Second Congress, 1903

The founding congress of the Russian Social-Democratic Labor Party (called the Second Congress because of an abortive affair in 1898) took place in 1903. This congress is best known for the Bolshevik-Menshevik split that took place during its long sessions. Plekhanov voted with Lenin on all the issues, and then, not long after, went over to the Mensheviks.

At this congress full of lively controversy, the vote on the program was near unanimous, including the point for which this congress was unique: the insertion of 'dictatorship of the proletariat' into the official party program. No other party had done this. The man who had played the largest role in drafting the program was the acknowledged theoretical leader of the movement, Plekhanov.★

The program formulated the idea in the terms that had now become standard: suppression of counterrevolution.

. . . the social revolution of the proletariat will put an end to the division of society into classes and thus will liberate all oppressed humanity as well as end all forms of exploitation of one part of society by another.

An essential condition for this social revolution is the dictatorship of the proletariat, i.e., the conquest by the proletariat of such political power as will enable it to quell all opposition by the exploiters.[13]

★Bertram Wolfe has written: "Latter-day Stalinist historians have stated that Plekhanov omitted the dictatorship of the proletariat from his draft program. This is not so, as an inspection of his draft will reveal."[12]—Both sides seem to be mistaken. According to Lenin's notes of 1902, it was a *second* draft program by Plekhanov that omitted the term, which had been in the first draft.[13] I presume (until someone who is competent clears up the matter) that the *Iskra* draft submitted to the congress reverted to the 'dictatorship of the proletariat,' right enough. Lenin's notes do not indicate the reason for Plekhanov's omission.

Plekhanov was the congress reporter on the program. The sole vote withheld from unanimous support came from Akimov, one of the extreme-reformist leaders of the "Economist" right wing. He objected to the entire program, not simply the 'dictatorship' plank. But there was discussion on the plank. The crux of most objections was not so much opposition to 'dictatorship' as to the revolutionary *Klang* of the term. The orthodox way to defend the term had become (as explained) to emphasize the need for the suppression of counter-revolution in order to preserve a *majority* revolution in the name of real democracy. Thus Trotsky's contribution to the debate (as quoted by Wolfe from the congress minutes) was entirely within this pattern:

> The rule of the working class was inconceivable until the great mass of them were united in desiring it. Then they would be an overwhelming majority. This would not be the dictatorship of a little band of conspirators or a minority party, but of the immense majority in the interests of the immense majority, to prevent counterrevolution. In short, it would represent the victory of true democracy.[14]

He assured objectors that the dictatorship of the proletariat was not "a Jacobin act."[15]

One of the delegates, a future Menshevik, thought ahead to what "dictatorship" might actually mean.* Mandelberg (pseudonym: Posadovsky) told the congress:

> The statements made here for and against the amendments [to the program] strike me as being not a dispute over details but a serious difference of opinion; without a doubt we disagree on the following fundamental question: Should our future policy be governed by certain basic democratic principles, admitted to have absolute value, or are all democratic principles to be governed exclusively by what is profitable for our party? I definitely declare for the latter. There is no democratic principle that we could not make subservient to the interests of our party. (*Interjection:* "Even inviolability of the person?") Yes! Inviolability of the person as well! As a revolutionary party striving towards its ultimate goal—that of a social revolution—we must regard democratic principles

---

*Wolfe and Dan write as if this discussion came up in the debate on the 'dictatorship of the proletariat' plank. According to J. L. H. Keep, the point under discussion was a two-year term for the future national assembly. According to Lenin's account, a few months after the congress, the occasion was the debate on proportional representation.[16]

exclusively from the point of view of the speediest possible achievement of that goal, from the point of view of our party's interests. If one or another demand does not turn out to our advantage we shall not use it. Therefore I oppose any amendments that are likely in future to narrow our freedom of action.[17]

J. L. H. Keep comments: "Neither before nor after was Mandelberg distinguished for his extremism. His call was essentially one for frankness: everyone should know what the Party really stood for."[18] One of the delegates rose to support Mandelberg; and his first name was not Vladimir. Plekhanov even went beyond Mandelberg, as he told the delegates that, while we support universal suffrage, "as revolutionaries we must say openly that we do not want to convert it into a fetish."[19]

> I fully support what Comrade Posadovsky has said. Every given democratic principle should be examined not on its own merits in the abstract, but in its bearing on what may be called the basic principle of democracy, namely, on the principle that says *Salus populi suprema lex* [The welfare of the people is the highest law]. Translated into the language of the revolutionary, this means that the success of the revolution is the highest law.

To interrupt for a moment: Translated into everybody's language, this is a rather crude form of the "end determines the means" fallacy; that is, it ignores the dialectical consideration that the means also condition the end, and that in any case a given end "determines" or points to only those means that really can be shown to lead to *that* end.[20] Plekhanov had scouted such considerations when he quoted them from Lavrov, and now he was simply blind to them. Granting that the interests of a revolution might momentarily infringe on one or another democratic principle or its application, it is rather misleading to call *this* the "basic principle of democracy" itself. Plekhanov turns the exception into the rule—in advance. Plekhanov's speech continued as follows:

> If it were necessary for the success of the revolution to restrict the effect of one or another democratic principle, it would be criminal to hesitate at such a restriction.* As my own personal opinion I would say that even the principle of universal suffrage should be regarded from the point of

---

*The English translation I am quoting here actually says at this point: ". . . it would be criminal to stop at such a restriction." This is unclear. The translations of this passage in Dan and Wolfe (reference-noted elsewhere) both say, "It would be a crime to hesitate."

view of this basic principle of democracy I have just mentioned. Hypothetically it is conceivable that we, Social-Democrats, may have occasion to come out against universal suffrage. The bourgeoisie of the Italian republics once deprived persons belonging to the nobility of political rights. The revolutionary proletariat could restrict the political rights of the upper classes the way these classes once restricted the political rights of the proletariat. The fitness of such a measure could only be judged by the rule *Salus revolutionis suprema lex.*

Plekhanov then applied his "principle" to representative assemblies in general:

The same point of view should be adopted by us on the question of the duration of parliaments. If, on an impulse of revolutionary enthusiasm, the people were to elect a very good parliament . . . we should try and make it a long parliament; and if the elections turned out to be unfavorable we should try and dismiss it not in two years' time but if possible in two weeks.[21]

It is easy to see why Lenin quoted this passage in early 1918.

Plekhanov's priority in explicitly conferring an antidemocratic content on the 'dictatorship of the proletariat' has been embarrassing for some historians of the Russian movement. Following are three ways to handle embarrassments of this sort.

(1) The easy way out, of course, is to omit all mention of the inconvenient facts. For example, Leonard Schapiro's *The Communist Party of the Soviet Union* devotes two pages to differences on the 'dictatorship of the proletariat' between Plekhanov and Lenin during the discussions *preceding* the 1903 congress, allegedly proving that Lenin, unlike Plekhanov, looked to a dictatorship over the peasant majority; but in his next six pages, on the congress itself, the question has disappeared.[22] Another piquant example is Martov's *History of the Russian Social-Democracy.* The chapter on the Second Congress mentions that there was some opposition to the 'dictatorship' plank, but is otherwise silent on the discussion that took place.[23]

(2) Theodore Dan, in his *Origins of Bolshevism,* resorts to falsification in order to remedy the inconveniences of history. "Plekhanov was the only one to support Posadovsky [Mandelberg]," he claims. And he adds: "in spite of all Plekhanov's authority, his and Posadovsky's position did not find the slightest support at the congress."[24]

Wolfe, with an eye on the congress minutes, unwittingly gives Dan the lie:

Plekhanov's remarks on the subordination of democratic principles to the needs of the revolution were interrupted by demonstrative applause. But there were hisses, too.[25]

When Lenin wrote *One Step Forward, Two Steps Back* less than a year after the congress, he was not exposing Dan's future fiction; he was simply giving some details about the episode, including the applause and the hisses. (He was in the chair at the time, according to Wolfe.) Lenin's account reported that Plekhanov's speech was greeted by applause and hissing. When an objection was made from the floor against the hissing, the right-winger Egorov rose to say, "Since such speeches call forth applause, I am obliged to hiss." In a later statement Martov took for granted that the approval of Plekhanov's statement was general but that "some of the delegates" were indignant at it.

Lenin wound up his account with the statement that *all* the Iskraists (i.e., future Mensheviks and Bolsheviks together) were favorable to the Posadovsky-Plekhanov view, as against the anti-Iskra center and right wing. Why, then, was Plekhanov "the only one to support Posadovsky" with a speech? Lenin's report answered this in advance without knowing that the question would be raised by Dan: "Unfortunately, the debate was closed" on the proportional-representation point (see footnote above, page 69) and so this side-point that had "cropped up in it immediately vanished" before anyone else could pursue the argument.[26]

The reason for Dan's falsifiction appears on the same page: he wishes to claim that "Lenin broke sharply with the quarter-of-a-century-old traditions of Russian Marxism."[27] We will find more about these "traditions" in the next section.

(3) Plekhanov's biographer Baron tries to make out that the 1903 statement was new for his man: "The Plekhanov who spoke these words appeared to have gravitated to the very position against which he had issued a solemn warning in *Our Differences*."[28] What did Plekhanov solemnly warn against in *Our Differences*? Baron was in fact referring to a "warning" by Plekhanov against "the ideals of 'patriarchal and authoritarian communism'" as represented by the Inca regime in Peru![29] Baron's biography had not even mentioned Plekhanov's statements about 'dictatorship of the proletariat' in *Our Differences*—statements which were not "against" but rather a preparation *for* the 1903 position taken by Plekhanov.

One other fact about Plekhanov needs mentioning; it is too well known to require documentation. This was Plekhanov's *personal* authoritarian and dictatorial style, particularly in relations with comrades. In all personal-political relations, Plekhanov could function only as absolute dictator. In such cases—and Plekhanov was an extreme case—there is no automatic carryover from the personal to the general-political, but it is certainly a relevant datum.[30]

3. The Mensheviks' 'Dictatorship'

The Mensheviks retained the 'dictatorship of the proletariat' in their party program after the Second Congress. Neither in 1903 nor after, neither by the Mensheviks nor the Bolsheviks, has anyone explained why the 'dictatorship of the proletariat' had to go into the party program *only* in the case of the Russian party, when even the much-admired German party did not do so.

Maybe it had something to do with the erroneous belief that Marx had proposed the inclusion in his "Critique of the Gotha Program"; but I do not find this argument alluded to. An easy speculation, of course, is that Russian conditions made the necessity of dictatorial measures an inevitable accompaniment of revolution, and that the absence of a bourgeois-democratic public of any size made it less costly to speak in 'dictatorial' terms.

We find a different reason given by the Menshevik theoreticians and historians Julius Martov and Theodore Dan. They have argued that the motivating factor was the need to repudiate Revisionism. Martov gave this account:

> Bernstein, Jaurès and other critics of Marxism insisted on giving the expression "dictatorship of the proletariat" the Blanquist definition of power held by an organized minority and resting on violence exercised by this minority over the majority. For this reason the authors of the Russian program were obliged to fix as narrowly as possible the limits of this political idea. They did that by declaring that the dictatorship of the proletariat is the power used by the proletariat to crush all resistance which the exploiting class might oppose to the realization of the socialist and revolutionary transformation. Simply that.
> *An effective force concentrated in the State, which can thus realize the conscious will of the majority despite the resistance of an economically powerful minority—here is the dictatorship of the proletariat.*[31]

Theodore Dan gave a similar explanation. In a 1932 lecture, looking back, he argued that the term could not be abandoned, since this might imply acceptance of Revisionist views:

> The negation of the 'dictatorship of the proletariat' is equivalent to the conception that democratic society would automatically grow into socialism, to the conception of the final disappearance of the revolutionary role of violence in the future course of the class struggle . . .[32]

His conclusion:

> And that is why our program—drawn up by Plekhanov and adopted unanimously in 1903, that is, at the time of the most ardent struggle between Revisionists and orthodoxers, at the London congress of our party, then still united—was the first of all the socialist programs to use the expression 'dictatorship of the proletariat.' In order to counter the attempts of the Revisionists to cast discredit on this idea by interpreting it in the Jacobin sense of a terrorist minority dictatorship, our program at the same time gave a precise definition of what was meant by this expression.[33] [The 1903 plank is quoted here.]

One difficulty with this argument is that it does not explain why this terminological repudiation of Revisionism had to go into the Russian party program, unlike other parties which repudiated Revisionism.

At the 1903 congress Martov did not repudiate Plekhanov's *Salus revolutionis* speech. As he wrote in 1919, he first tried to convince himself that Plekhanov did not really believe what he had said, but—

> In a private conversation with me, Plekhanov objected to my putting such an interpretation on his words. I understood then that his conception of the dictatorship of the proletariat was not free of a certain kinship with the *Jacobin dictatorship by a revolutionary minority*.[34]

Martov's repudiation came in October 1903, at the Geneva congress of émigré Social-Democratic groups. His biographer relates:

> He reproved Plekhanov for his cynical rejection of democratic principles at the party congress and told him that he should at least have added that "so tragic a situation was unthinkable as one in which the proletariat to consolidate its victory would have to violate such political rights as, e.g., the freedom of the press." Plekhanov, unimpressed, replied with a laconic "Merci!"[35]

Plekhanov's laconic reply was hardly brilliant; but by this time, when he was just in the process of turning his coat, he may have found that it was pinching a little. Martov's proposal—to dispose of a question you're thinking about by saying it is "unthinkable"—was not exactly brilliant either. Both of these leading Marxist theoreticians felt extremely uncomfortable about the whole thing.

Theodore Dan later faced up to another question about the 1903 episode. He wrote about Plekhanov's *Salis revolutionis* speech that

> it was typical of the general intellectual mood of "Menshevism," only just beginning to become a distinct entity, that it was precisely two future Mensheviks who championed the idea concerning the absolute subordination of the Party's politico-democratic objectives to its proletarian-socialist objectives that twelve to thirteen years later became the fundamental dogma of "Bolshevism in power," which it began to fulfill by dispersing the Constituent Assembly.[36]

Unfortunately, Dan does not explain what this "general intellectual mood" was that made budding Menshevism identical in a "fundamental dogma" with devilish Bolshevism.

The Menshevik party retained 'dictatorship of the proletariat' in its party program long after the revolution of 1917, while distinguishing its interpretation from that of Leninism. In the theses drawn up by Martov and adopted by the Mensheviks' 1922 congress, the 'dictatorship of the proletariat' was said to be "the violence organized by the state" against the parasitic capitalist minority "to the extent that the latter tries to resist the social revolution," but this power, it was emphasized, must never be directed against other strata of the working classes and never imposed on a majority.[37]

4. Some Other Russians

Although 'dictatorship of the proletariat' was accepted into the program by almost all wings of the Russian party, it figured prominently in their factional divisions. But, as is often the case, its role here was that of a code word. The political divisions that separated Mensheviks from Bolsheviks, and Trotsky from both, were not simply terminological; they were based on fundamental differences in approach to the question of questions: the nature of the coming revolution—bourgeois, proletarian, or what?

This question is the subject of innumerable books: here we wish only to indicate how the term as such was related to the controversy. For the Mensheviks, the Provisional Revolutionary Government would have to be a bourgeois-democratic government for a whole period; for Lenin, the revolutionary government would be a 'revolutionary democratic dictatorship of the proletariat and peasantry,' in which an alliance of the two classes would (somehow) be the ruling power; for Trotsky, it could be nothing but a 'dictatorship of the proletariat,' albeit *supported* by other working classes, especially the peasantry.

For all three tendencies, as laid down in the 1903 program, the 'dictatorship' aspect of the perspective involved the necessity for suppressing counterrevolutionary forces. The difference between Trotsky and Lenin, expressed in a terminological disagreement, entailed a basic difference in policy: could the new revolutionary regime take directly *socialist* measures (basic inroads on private property) without breaking the alliance with the peasantry? By calling for a 'dictatorship of the proletariat,' Trotsky said yes. By inventing the hitherto unknown 'dictatorship of the proletariat and peasantry,' Lenin said no. By opposing the application of the 'dictatorship of the proletariat' to the provisional government, the Mensheviks made clear it had to be a *bourgeois*-democratic government—or, speaking scientifically, a 'bourgeois dictatorship.'

In this sense the varying 'dictatorship' formulations were simply shorthand expressions for the underlying programmatic disagreements. The term 'hegemony' was thrown in too, but its relationship to 'dictatorship' was not fixed. Thus J. L. H. Keep says that in the late 1890s Axelrod (who later became a leading Menshevik) put forward the view "that the proletariat should exercise 'hegemony' (as distinct from dictatorship) during the first phase of revolution."[38] The crux is in the parenthetical clause. 'Hegemony' simply referred to the doctrine accepted by all Russian Marxists that it was the task of the proletariat to take the leadership of the revolutionary classes; and Keep's report is of interest only if Axelrod really counterposed 'hegemony' to 'dictatorship.'

On the other hand, at the party's "unification congress" in Stockholm in April 1906, a Bolshevik delegate named "Ivanovich" also spoke of "hegemony":

"Either the hegemony of the proletariat . . . or the hegemony of the democratic bourgeoisie . . ." In the event of the complete victory of the revolution, that "hegemony" must naturally lead to the dictatorship of the proletariat, with all its implied consequences.[39]

So reports Trotsky, who says that "Ivanovich" (aka Stalin) was merely paraphrasing Lenin. It would appear that this "hegemony" of the proletariat meant merely the leading role of the proletariat in the revolution, and would "naturally *lead* to the dictatorship of the proletariat" when the revolution won power. There were other terms around, like the "autocracy of the people,"[40] but these did not really advance the question.

As for Trotsky himself before 1917: we do not find that he used 'dictatorship' in any manner different from his faction opponents. It is true that he attacked Lenin for instituting a bureaucratic and personal dictatorship *within* the movement; this came in his violent denunciation of Lenin's "substitutionism" in *Our Political Tasks* in 1904: the organization of the party at first substitutes itself for the party as a whole—the Central Committee substitutes itself for the former—"and finally a single 'dictator' substitutes himself for the Central Committee . . ."[41] But while this offered a pejorative interpretation of what Lenin was doing, the *terms* of the indictment were exactly the same as everyone else's. "A proletariat capable of exercising its dictatorship over society," he argued, "will not tolerate any dictatorship over itself . . ."[42] In this sentence the two 'dictatorships' are used coordinately, as if referring to the same thing: here the very sentence structure incarnates the "misunderstanding."

Two years later, Trotsky summed up his theory of permanent revolution in a pamphlet based on the experience of 1905:

> *Without direct political aid from the European proletariat the working class of Russia will not be able to retain its power and to turn its temporary supremacy into a permanent Socialist dictatorship. . . .* On the other hand, there is no doubt that a *Socialist revolution in the West would allow us to turn the temporary supremacy of the working class directly into a Socialist dictatorship.*[43]

There is a problem about this formulation. According to it, the Russian working class *in power* needs a revolution in the West before it can turn its "temporary supremacy" into—something else, which Trotsky calls "a permanent Socialist dictatorship." Then the "temporary supremacy," maintained for some length of time, is *not* a proletarian dictatorship? (This makes no sense in terms of Trotsky's views.) Or if it is, then what exactly is this *later* "permanent Socialist dictatorship"? A couple of other questions crowd in. The movement had not talked in terms of a *'socialist* dictatorship' but of a class dictatorship. And calling it "permanent" was the exact opposite of the usual appellation, which was "temporary."

Clearly Trotsky was using the term 'dictatorship' with more than its now customary looseness.

So far we have been considering the tendencies inside the Social-Democratic Party. But 'dictatorship,' as we know, was no invention of the Social-Democrats; ideas about the establishment of a dictatorship were standard fixtures in the older Russian movement, from Bakunin to Tkachev and the revolutionary Narodniks, who were well aware of the difficulties of thinking in terms of self-government by the dark peasant masses. By the twentieth century, the heirs of the Narodnik movement were organized in the Socialist Revolutionary Party, which held its first congress in 1906.

The S.R. program sanctioned resort to dictatorship. For information on this, we have to turn to O. H. Radkey, who is to the S.R.'s what Dommanget is to Blanqui: that is, an honest and scholarly historian who tries to act as defense attorney for his adopted subject without going outside the bounds of truth. In both cases, sometimes the defense-attorney operation makes it a little difficult to pick out the bits of truth.

Radkey writes of the 1906 program:

> In case of need, the program expressly sanctioned the resort to a "temporary revolutionary dictatorship." Some members of the party, not liking the connotations of the word "dictatorship" under any circumstances, argued that this implied the manifest absurdity of the people's establishing a dictatorship over itself; but Chernov, citing the example of the French Revolution and Thiers's regime in 1871, maintained that recourse to dictatorial methods on the part of a majority was by no means unknown to history, and that it was necessary to have a reliable weapon in the arsenal of socialism for use against the plottings and intrigue of the dispossessed minority.[44]

Radkey adds that the program actually spoke of a dictatorship of the "working class," but that Chernov used "working class" as synonymous with the "people." Radkey argues that the S.R. formula "differed widely" from Lenin's because it "envisaged no departure from democracy until the hour of the definitive triumph of socialism, when dictatorship would serve merely as a temporary expedient of the majority, to be laid aside as soon as the immediate purpose had been achieved," at which time "dictatorial methods could be discarded, safely and with dispatch (in theory, at any rate) . . ."[45]

One must assume that the phrase "until the hour of the definitive triumph of socialism means: "until the victory of the socialist revolution, that is, the taking of power," even though, taken literally, it means the triumphant achievement of a socialist society at the *end* of a transition period, at which point a dictatorship would cease to make sense. The former interpretation does make sense, since it envisions "departure[s] from democracy" after the taking of power, when the "dictatorship" has been installed; but it is not clear, then, why Chernov thought this differed from Lenin's view. (We leave aside the fact that it was Plekhanov who up to then had done most of the talking about postrevolutionary departures from democracy.)

At the 1906 founding congress the right wing was for its own kind of dictatorship, not Chernov's. This position was taken by V. V. Rudnev, the future mayor of Moscow, who argued for an extreme national-chauvinist point of view that rejected the right of self-determination for (say) the Finns and the Poles. Rudnev orated at the congress:

> More than that. The [coming] Great Russian Revolution has a great world task to perform, a transcending mission for all of humanity, in the name of which it has the right of revolutionary dictatorship—the right to violate the guarantees of peoples—and not only of those peoples associated by fate with Russia, but also of those elsewhere throughout the world.[46]

Rudnev, we see, has picked up the phrase 'revolutionary dictatorship,' but its content is simply the imperialist domination of subject peoples by the Russian state: reactionary pan-Slavism.

4
Lenin and 'Dictatorship'

As we have seen, in the social-democratic party in which Lenin grew up the 'dictatorship of the proletariat' was accepted by almost everyone. What did Lenin come to understand by the term?

Like everyone else, Lenin had to ask himself what Marx could have meant. By the time he started writing on socialist problems (the first writings in his *Collected Works* stem from 1893) the word 'dictatorship' had already acquired some of its modern meaning; it was even beginning to be counterposed to 'democracy' to some extent. Yet Lenin, like other Marxists, assumed that the historical fate of socialism was inextricably linked to the advance of democracy, social, economic and political: "Whoever wants to reach socialism by any other path than that of political democracy will inevitably arrive at conclusions that are absurd and reactionary both in the economic and political sense."[1]

The rather surprising outcome was that Lenin worked out for himself, or invented, a unique definition of 'dictatorship' which, as far as I know, came out of his own head. More than ever, different people discussing 'dictatorship of the proletariat' were using a different vocabulary, talking past each other.

Throughout Lenin's writings—as in Luxemburg's and others'—there were passages of curt reference to the 'dictatorship of the proletariat' which simply connected it up with the generic concept of 'conquest of power.' The best example of this came in Lenin's *Granat Encyclopaedia* article "Karl Marx," written in 1914; it routinely referred to

a political struggle directed towards the conquest of political power by the proletariat ("the dictatorship of the proletariat").[2]

But these passages are unedifying. We want to pause at those that revealed what the writer thought the term meant.

1. First Interpretation

For the first decade of Lenin's literary activity, from 1893 up to 1902, there is no record that he used the term at all. He must have seen it in Plekhanov's writings, in Bernstein's attack, in Kautsky, etc., but it played no role in his own formulations.

Test cases are provided by the drafts for party programs that he did in the 1890s. In 1895–1896 he wrote such a draft, plus an "Explanation of the Program," but in both documents the passages dealing with state power made no use of the term.[3] Near the end of 1899 he wrote another piece on what a draft party program should say—with similar results.[4] About the same time, an unpublished review-essay on Kautsky's *Anti-Bernstein* discussed the Revisionist case; Bernstein's remarks on the 'dictatorship of the proletariat' did not figure in it.[5]

In fact Lenin paid no attention whatever to the term 'dictatorship of the proletariat' or 'dictatorship' alone until the question was imposed on the Russian movement by Plekhanov in 1902. This underlines from another side that it was Plekhanov who was the begetter, *fons et origo,* of the career of 'dictatorship of the proletariat' in the socialist movement.

In early 1902, preparing for the Second Congress of the Russian Social-Democratic Workers Party, Plekhanov (as we have seen in the preceding chapter) included 'dictatorship of the proletariat' in a draft for the party program. The fight against Bernsteinian Revisionism, in its West European and Russian forms, had heated up, too. In his main precongress discussion piece, *What Is To Be Done?,* Lenin was mainly interested in other problems; and while 'dictatorship of the proletariat' occurred three times in this work, the references were routine ones, as it were. That is, the formulations were such incidental references to workers' political power that one cannot say if they entailed any special understanding of the term.[6]

Among Lenin's papers of the time we find an "Outline of Plekhanov's First Draft Program," in which one of the planks used "command of political power" simply in apposition with 'dictatorship of the proletariat.'[7] In a draft program drawn up together with other *Iskra* editors, a plank linked up 'dictatorship of the proletariat' with defense of the revolution in the usual manner.[8]

It was in his "Notes on Plekhanov's Second Draft Program," jotted down in February–March, that we get the first indication of how Lenin understood the term. It transpired that he understood it to refer *only* to the suppressive tasks of a workers' government.

His argument went as follows: if the (Russian) petty-bourgeoisie, including the peasantry, *supported* the proletariat in the revolution, then of course it would not need to be suppressed, and therefore *a "dictatorship" could be dispensed with*. This thought explains the following notes:

> . . . the concept of "dictatorship" is incompatible with *positive* recognition of the outside support for the proletariat. If we really knew *positively* that the petty-bourgeoisie will support the proletariat in the accomplishment of its, the proletariat's, revolution it would be pointless to speak of a "dictatorship," for we would then be fully guaranteed so overwhelming a majority that we could get on very well without a dictatorship (as the "critics" [Revisionists] would have us believe).

The next sentence tries an interpretation of Marx:

> The recognition of the necessity for the dictatorship of the proletariat is *most closely and inseparably* bound up with the thesis of the *Communist Manifesto* that the proletariat *alone* is a really revolutionary class.[9]

This was a remarkable blunder. It was in the Manifesto, which indeed did assert that "the proletariat alone is a really revolutionary class,"[10] that Marx on the next page viewed the socialist movement as the "independent movement of the immense majority, in the interests of the immense majority."[11] In any case Marx was convinced that the socialist revolution would *normally* come about with the support of a secure majority of the masses of people. According to Lenin's 1902 notes, this would mean that a "dictatorship" of the proletariat would be unnecessary. In short, the 'dictatorship of the proletariat' *ceased to be applicable to the advanced capitalist countries* and became a special institution relevant mainly to countries like Russia.

It goes without saying, in the light of the evidence, that this view has no resemblance to Marx's. Indeed, it has no resemblance to any subsequent claim made by Lenin about the *international* applicability of the concept. Asking himself why a democratically-based popular revolution should be called a 'dictatorship,' Lenin had adopted Plekhanov's solution. Plekhanov's contribution to the puzzle had been to spell out the antidemocratic meaning of the term. Lenin's notes carried this approach to a logical conclusion—and therefore to a theoretical disaster, in which the explanation ceased even to make good sense. To be sure, this had taken place before Plekhanov spoke at the Second Congress; but Lenin's notes were based on a discussion of Plekhanov's advance drafts, and Plekhanov no doubt argued for them at least as frankly in *Iskra* discussions as he did at the congress sessions.

How far along the road Lenin's thinking carried the matter can be seen in a further note, a couple of pages on. It was addressed to the peasants, pitched in terms of how much "indulgence" a workers' state could show to them if they behaved properly:

> Now then, we say, if you adopt this, our, standpoint [as given in the theoretical part of the party program], you can count on "indulgence" of every kind, but if you don't, well then, don't get angry with us! Under the "dictatorship" we shall say about you: there is no point in wasting words where the use of power is required.[12]

Very tough-talking, to be sure, and the more mature Lenin would consider such an attitude very stupid. It occurred only in private notes, and was not repeated. But it left no doubt about what the writer thought "the dictatorship" was all about. It was about the Plekhanov-type *abrogation of democratic rights in specific situations* and nothing else.

If Lenin did not subsequently recur to this view that a 'dictatorship of the proletariat' would be *unnecessary* if a secure majority were assured to a workers' state, this was true no doubt because it was so utterly untenable in theoretical terms. He was going to have to invent a different solution to the problem.

2. The Two-Class "Dictatorship"

At the Second Congress in 1903, Lenin did not participate in the brief discussion precipitated by Mandelberg and Plekhanov; as he explained, the point was cut short in the proceedings. But he had a word to say about it in his book on the congress split, *One Step Forward, Two Steps Back,* published in the spring of 1904.

Here he was especially interested in explaining how the congress divided into political tendencies. It was in illustrating this lineup that he twice mentioned the Mandelberg-Plekhanov speeches. [13] Not because he felt he had to vindicate them: he reported that they were not controversial among the Iskraists, and this indeed was the significance he saw in the episode, since it showed once again that the Right and Center were ranged against the revolutionary social-democracy.

Lenin's brochure, therefore, offered no substantive discussion of the issue, since it assumed that Plekhanov's views were the generally accepted views of Marxists. He did not betray awareness that an issue existed.

In another year the revolution of 1905 changed the entire political landscape, and precipitated efforts by the socialist leaders to rethink the problems of the Russian revolution. We have already mentioned (Chapter 3, Section 4) that Lenin came up with a watchword which he formulated as the "revolutionary-democratic dictatorship of the proletariat and the peasantry." This presented two terminological problems.

(1) How could one have a "dictatorship" of two classes? If in Marx's terms a class 'dictatorship' meant simply the possession of state power by a given class (as in a 'dictatorship of the bourgeoisie' exercised in, say, a parliamentary democracy like England), then a proletarian-cum-peasant 'dictatorship' would mean a state in which two quite different classes were simultaneously in power. Marx would have found it hard to make sense of this.

Actually, the term was invented by Lenin, early in 1905, without regard to this theoretical difficulty, but in response to the political dilemma of the revolution. The Russian proletariat was small and economically weak in this backward country, but politically decisive in organizing and leading the revolutionary upsurge against the autocracy, an upsurge mainly powered by the peasant masses. The proletariat could be envisioned by the socialists as playing a "hegemonic" (leading) role in the revolution itself; but if, on the crest of revolt, it formed the expected "Provisional Revolutionary Government," could it really establish and maintain a workers' state? Workers' state—this meant moving toward governmental measures that went beyond bourgeois property relations, *socialist* measures. If it took socialist measures, it would alienate mass peasant support to the revolution. Lenin's solution was to propose that the Provisional Revolutionary Government to be established on the downfall of the autocracy should be based on an *alliance* of the two revolutionary classes; and while the workers' (socialist) representatives in the alliance would play the leading role ("hegemony of the proletariat") they would have to confine the action of the government in an essential respect. This government would carry through the democratization of Russian society (the "bourgeois-democratic revolution") to its most extreme end, but would refrain from taking directly socialist measures, measures encroaching on the private-property rights that defined capitalism.

It is not our present task, fortunately, to discuss the merits and demerits of this solution of Lenin's to the crucial problem of the Russian revolution. As we saw, Trotsky argued that a Provisional Revolutionary Government would not be able to refrain from socialist measures, and hence would be compelled to act as a workers' state, even if one which made maximum efforts to satisfy peasant needs. What Lenin was trying to emphasize, with his newly invented term, was that the proposed Provisional Revolutionary Government would have to be (1) an alliance of the two classes (2) which could *not* carry out a socialist program, even if led by socialists.

As is well known, Trotsky's prediction was more or less verified in 1917 by Lenin's own government, which in fact was compelled to take socialist measures. The two-class 'dictatorship' never came into living existence, and it is perhaps unfruitful to speculate whether such a societal beast could ever have been viable. Lenin's two-class 'dictatorship' remained an ideological construct, and today has a museumlike quality.

What, then, was the point of calling this construct a *'dictatorship'* of two classes? It was a good example of the "tyranny of language"—language forms imposing themselves in a terminological "logic" regardless of other logical relations. The "logic" went this way. If the Provisional Revolutionary Government was not going to be a 'dictatorship of the proletariat' in accordance with the Russian party program, it had to be some other 'dictatorship.' The code-word became the language; 'revolutionary government' had to be translated into 'revolutionary dictatorship.' Besides, if 'dictatorship' entailed suppression (as everyone thought), who was going to suppress whom?

The two-class 'dictatorship' was a way of promising (terminologically) that the revolutionary government would not suppress the peasantry.

(2) The other terminological problem was the affixation of 'democratic' before this 'dictatorship.' This development has been mentioned before: here 'democratic' was a short form of 'bourgeois-democratic,' and Lenin's watchword meant that the Provisional Revolutionary Government would confine itself to the tasks of the bourgeois-democratic revolution.

We have seen[14] that in Western Europe in mid-century the term 'Democracy' (as in '*the* Democracy') had gone through a course of development: at first, a broad term for the left opponents of absolutism, including both bourgeois-democrats and proletarian-socialist democrats; later, especially after 1849, a term eschewed by the revolutionary left, which used it pejoratively to mean pinkish radicals and social-democratic liberals. In Russia, where there was a great deal of catching up to do, the term 'democratic' hardened, in socialist usage, into a virtual synonym for 'bourgeois-democratic' as distinct from *or opposed to* 'socialist.' (This usage was not unknown in the West even by the turn of the century, but it was less consistent.)

Terminologically, this development was explicable; in political thinking, it was an invitation to a muddle. If 'democratic' implied 'bourgeois,' then socialists who wanted to be "revolutionary" were led to say it only with a sneer or grimace. One aspect of the muddle to which it led was the (later) growing belief, in some left circles and among some self-styled revolutionary Marxists, that 'democracy' had *no* meaning except in terms of class power.

Thus Lenin's "slogan" of the "democratic dictatorship" of the two revolutionary classes made its appearance in a context which put the main stress not on the 'dictatorship' but focused controversy on the other ingredients—the limitation promised by 'democratic' and the two-class problem stated by the "proletariat and the peasantry."

Lenin's "slogan" *could* have been formulated without the word 'dictatorship' *and often was so formulated by Lenin himself:* e.g., a "revolutionary proletarian-peasant government," etc. The ironic fact is that the impetus, or occasion, for formulating it around the word 'dictatorship' came from outside Lenin: it came from his Menshevik opponents. (This may remind us how the question of dictatorship was raised at the Second Congress not by Lenin but by two future Mensheviks.)

To see what happened, let us pinpoint exactly when Lenin started using the 'democratic dictatorship' slogan and under what circumstances. Even before the 1905 revolution he had already adumbrated the underlying idea of a proletarian-peasant alliance in a revolutionary government. But when did he start attaching the term 'dictatorship' to this germinal idea?

The answer is: it was linked to Lenin's response to the Mensheviks' publication of a pamphlet by the leading Menshevik A. S. Martynov. Martynov's pamphlet was entitled *Two Dictatorships*. During the first months of 1905 Lenin referred to and quoted from this pamphlet numerous times, as a punching-bag. What he kept on quoting was a passage in which Martynov *denounced* the idea of the socialist party's bringing about a successful popular uprising against the autocracy, because this victory would force it to assume power and (horrors!) institute a proletarian dictatorship, when all Mensheviks knew that only a bourgeois regime was in the cards. The modern reader must keep in mind that Martynov's horror was not evoked by 'dictatorship' but by 'proletarian,' that is, the error was to institute a proletarian-socialist regime under premature conditions which made survival impossible in backward Russia.

Lenin's first publication of the 'democratic dictatorship' formula came in an issue of his paper (March 8, 1905) in which he polemized against Martynov's pamphlet and propounded the brand-new slogan.* All through these early months of 1905, when we find the very

---

*A month before, Lenin's papers show notes for a draft resolution intended for the Third Congress of the party, in which he listed positions taken by the Mensheviks showing their rightward shift; and last on this list was their rejection of the idea of "the revolutionary-democratic dictatorship of the proletariat and the petty-bourgeoisie" in the revolution.[15] So he was already thinking of it. In the March 8 issue of his organ *Vperyod,* he had two articles: in one he mentioned the Mensheviks' "fear of the revolutionary-democratic dictatorship of the proletariat and the peasantry" much as in his notes; in the other article he made clear that the charge of "fear" was based on the Martynov pamphlet, which he polemized against. Martynov, he said, tries to frighten workers "with the dire perspective of participation in the provisional government and the 'revolutionary dictatorship' in a *democratic* revolution . . ."[16] From here on, his use of the 'democratic dictatorship' formula comes in connection with further polemics against Martynov's *Two Dictatorships*.

first uses of the 'democratic dictatorship of the proletariat and the peasantry,' virtually every use is in connection with a response to Martynov's *Two Dictatorships.*

Then at the Third Congress, Lenin made this connection himself, eliminating any possibility of doubt about the immediate genesis of the formula. The party congress met in April–May; Lenin reported on Social-Democratic participation in a Provisional Revolutionary Government. He began the report by saying that this question of participation did *not* come up because the prospect was imminent. Why then did it come up?

> But the question has been forced upon us not so much by the actual state of affairs as by literary polemics. It must always be borne in mind that the question was first raised by Martynov, and that he raised it *before January 9* [Bloody Sunday]. He wrote in his pamphlet *Two Dictatorships . . .* [17]

And he proceeded to quote the same passage from Martynov's pamphlet that he had been attacking ever since February, and he likewise proceeded to put forward the 'democratic dictatorship' formula once again, his response to Martynov.

3. The New Definition

Lenin's exposition of the two-class dictatorship "slogan" began with the April 12, 1905, issue of his paper, and was continued in the discussions and documents of the Third Congress. [18] The reader can find accounts of the subsequent controversy in many works. If we keep an eye specifically on our own narrower question—the meaning assigned to 'dictatorship' in the controversy—we find the usual lack of awareness about the existence of the problem. But in fact Lenin was incubating a new interpretation of the meaning of the word.

The new meaning was dimly adumbrated in his aforementioned report to the Third Congress. There he said, of the "revolutionary dictatorship":

> It can be only a dictatorship, that is, not an organization of "order," but an organization of war. If you are storming a fortress, you cannot discontinue the war even after you have taken the fortress. [19]

In his major work of this period, *Two Tactics of the Social-Democracy,* the incubation period had not yet terminated, but he made another point of the utmost importance, on an aspect of the problem that would remain for a long time. After exploring Marx's statements about 'dictatorship' in 1848,[20] he was moved to stress that 'dictatorship' and 'democracy' are not "mutually exclusive." It was a conclusion he was going to find hard to remember:

> . . . the bourgeoisie understands by dictatorship the annulment of all liberties and guarantees of democracy, arbitrariness of every kind, and every sort of abuse of power in a dictator's personal interests.[21]

This was the "vulgar bourgeois view," he wrote. What was *his* view? From Marx's 1848 articles he gathered that "the task of such a [revolutionary] dictatorship is to destroy the remnants of the old institutions." But what is "dictatorial" about *that,* given a democratically based revolution? He had not yet incubated an answer. When the Mensheviks objected to his two-class 'dictatorship' formula on the ground that dictatorship presupposes a "single will," he did not reject the *definition,* but merely argued that it was "abstract."[22] This argument was not about the will of a single man but of a single class.

His own definition of 'dictatorship' was ready for publication less than a year later. In April 1906 he published a pamphlet, *The Victory of the Cadets and the Tasks of the Workers' Party,* which presented it fullpanoplied.* For the first time by anybody in a long while, this work showed awareness that there was a problem about the common understanding of the word 'dictatorship.'

> Why "dictatorship," why "force"? . . .
> This question is usually put by people who for the first time hear the term 'dictatorship' used in what to them is a new connotation. People are accustomed to see only a police authority and only a police dictatorship. The idea that there can be a government without any police, or that dictatorship need not be a police dictatorship, seems strange to them.[24]

This is a fresh and welcome note in our study, an insight for which Lenin was well nigh unique in this period. Unfortunately, the positive content of this work was less happy. For, after cogitating over the

---

*The importance of this work was underlined by the fact that in October 1920 Lenin published a long study titled *A Contribution to the History of the Question of the Dictatorship,* which consisted mainly of a fifteen-page-long reprint from the 1906 pamphlet.[23]

problem of just why 'dictatorship' was dictatorial, he had worked out an answer which must produce more puzzlement than enlightenment.

His target here was the mildly liberal-reform Constitutional Democratic Party (Cadets, for short), whose "professors" were misrepresenting the views of the revolutionaries, he said. "Please note," he told them,

> that dictatorship means unlimited power based on force, and not on law. In civil war, any victorious power can only be a dictatorship.[25]

This was not an incidental thought; he repeated it. The soviets that had arisen in 1905, he said, were the embryo of a new revolutionary government; they

> represented a dictatorship in embryo, for they recognized *no* other authority, *no* law and *no* standards, no matter by whom established. Authority—unlimited, outside the law, and based on force in the most direct sense of the word—is dictatorship.[26]

And he kept on insisting on it. He gave an example: suppose police were torturing a revolutionist, and a crowd of workers poured in and overwhelmed the torturers. "When a revolutionary people . . . resorts to force" against the "Cossacks"—

> that is a dictatorship of the revolutionary people. It is a *dictatorship,* because it is the authority of the people over [the Crossacks, etc.], an authority unrestricted by any laws . . .

He waxed "scientific":

> The scientific term "dictatorship" means nothing more nor less than authority untrammeled by any laws, absolutely unrestricted by any rules whatever, and based directly on force. The term "dictatorship" *has no other meaning but this* . . .[27]

This definition of 'dictatorship' was going to be held and expounded by Lenin for a long time, but it was already fully developed in this, its first exposition.

This definition can only be called a theoretical disaster, first-class, like Lenin's 1902 blunder. This reign of pure force, in which there existed no law, authority, standard, or rules "whatever," could exist, if at all, only for a relatively brief period of pitched battle, before the revolutionary forces won out and established their own state (or else lost, of course). Actually, even in a pitched battle it is unlikely that there will be *no* authorities, laws, etc.; on the contrary, there are likely to be a double set of these; but for the sake of argument let us concede that Lenin's no-law situation exists for the period of unresolved battle. But after?

If we are talking about a 'dictatorship of the proletariat,' victory in the battle means that a workers' state *begins* to operate. It must, to be sure, defend itself, suppress counterrevolution, recast the state institutions, etc.—in short, carry out all the tasks of a workers' state, whatever one conceives these to be; but it *begins* to operate. Without any laws whatever? Without rules? Without standards? On the contrary, its operation means that it establishes its own, new, class-reoriented laws, rules, standards and authorities, new institutions under its own law. According to Lenin's definition, as soon as it does so, the 'dictatorship' *ceases;* according to everyone else, the new workers' state *begins*.

As a matter of fact, although Lenin kept repeating this definition, he never drew the absurd conclusion that the 'dictatorship of the proletariat' ceased when a workers' state established its own laws and institutions. His definition lived on as a construct only.

Another remarkable aspect was Lenin's repeated claim that his definition was "scientific." This might suggest that he had encountered some allegedly scientific (e.g., philological, etc.) basis for the claim; but if he did, he never mentioned it. What is also puzzling is that he repeatedly referred to the "Latin" origin of the term 'dictatorship'[28]— yet did not appear to have an inkling of what the Latin (Roman) meaning really was; he did not even vouchsafe an incorrect inkling.

Whether he found the new definition in some unnamed source or invented it out of the blue, his definition of 'dictatorship' had nothing in common with any other conception of the term held by socialists or—what is more important—with any conception of the workers' state held by Marxists.

Now this sort of thing was not typical of Lenin, and a working hypothesis for such occasions is that the otherwise singular definition must have fulfilled some theoretical function for him despite its extreme weakness. If we ask what this function might have been, we need not go further to find it than the same article that first expounded the definition.

We have to go back to Lenin's example of the "dictatorship of the revolutionary people" who overwhelmed the police torturers: he drew the example out further. In this scene we see the dictatorship *of the people,* because the people, the mass of the population, unorganized, "casually" assembled at the given spot, itself appears on the scene, exercises justice and metes out punishment, exercises power and creates a new, revolutionary law.[29]

Parenthetically, we point out that if it created a new "law," it was *ipso facto* no longer a 'dictatorship,' according to the definition; but Lenin ignored this crying contradiction. Also: if we were to discuss the case more seriously, we would have to ask why a lynch mob is not also a 'dictatorship of the people,' and the answer would likewise burst the seams of Lenin's definition. But let us continue with Lenin's passage in order to see where he is going:

> Lastly, it is the dictatorship of the *revolutionary* people. Why only of the revolutionary, and not of the whole people? Because among the whole people, constantly suffering, and most cruelly, from the brutalities of the [Cossacks], there are some who are physically cowed and terrified . . .

And there are others who are "degraded" by bad theories that prevent them from fighting or "by prejudice, habit, routine"; and there are still others who stay out of the fight for one bad reason or another, including cowardice. Conclusion?

> That is why the dictatorship is exercised, not by the whole people, but by the revolutionary people who, however, do not shun the whole people, who explain to all the people the motives of their actions in all their details, and who willingly enlist the *whole* people not only in "administering" the state, but in governing it too, and indeed in organizing the state.
>
> Thus our simple analogy contains *all the elements* of the scientific concept "dictatorship of the revolutionary people," and also of the concept "military and police dictatorship."[30]

Thus the entire concept of a *class* dictatorship, whether of one or two classes, has been argued away by dint of a "scientific" definition, and *replaced* with the concept of an ad-hoc "dictatorship" wielded by the "revolutionary people"—a concept which Lenin's detailed example has made into a dictatorship wielded by *revolutionary activists.* This category obviously stands for the revolutionary party.

The entire construct has led to the transmogrification of the class dictatorship into a party dictatorship. Which was exactly what the traditional 'revolutionary dictatorship' had always meant to the movement before Marx: Q.E.D. The party dictatorship would, of course, "explain," "enlist," and refrain from "shunning" the "whole people." Here, though not subsequently, Lenin even forgot to mention that there were *classes* in between the "revolutionary people" (party) on the one hand and the "whole people" on the other.

It will be asserted, naturally, that this was a special "Leninist" distortion of the 'dictatorship of the proletariat' into the dictatorship of the party. But as we have pointed out, everyone else (with the possible later exception of Luxemburg) assumed that the 'dictatorship of the proletariat' would be exercised in practice as a 'dictatorship of the party.' They *assumed* it, but Lenin characteristically had to develop a reasoned basis for the idea. This is what he tried to do, and this was the sad result. But the conception that linked 'dictatorship of the proletariat' and 'dictatorship of the party' was not his invention.

4. *On State and Revolution*

With the decline of the revolutionary wave, the discussion of revolutionary problems also ebbed. There was a long hiatus, lasting into the period of World War I, in the incidence of Lenin's mentions of 'dictatorship of the proletariat.' In December 1906 there was an article in which he referred to the new definition of 'dictatorship': it was given in bare-bones fashion in two words, "unrestricted power." Outside of routine usages, there was an article in 1909 which stated that "the Bolsheviks have never spoken of the 'inevitability' of 'dictatorship' but of its necessity . . ."[31] The meaning is unclear but not worth the space to untangle.

The first year in which we find Lenin again referring repeatedly to the 'dictatorship of the proletariat' or to the two-class 'dictatorship' was 1916. The context was mainly the lively debate then going on among the Bolsheviks themselves on the question of the right of national self-determination. The connection between this question and 'dictatorship' was not direct; the references may have started cropping up simply because Lenin was studying the problems that led to the writing of *State and Revolution*.

Now in discussing the question of national self-determination Lenin's heavy emphasis was that self-determination was a *democratic* demand that had to be supported by socialists; and more than once he wanted to stress that this democratic demand, like democratic demands in general, was not incompatible with the programmatic concept of the 'dictatorship of the proletariat':*

> . . . socialism can be implemented only *through* the dictatorship of the proletariat, which combines violence against the bourgeoisie, i.e., the minority of the population, with *full* development of democracy, i.e., the genuinely equal and genuinely universal participation of the *entire* mass of the population in all *state* affairs and in all the complex problems of abolishing capitalism.[33]

This statement of the issue was close to Marx's concept; Lenin's espousal of national self-determination as a democratic issue seemed to turn his emphasis in that direction. It produced this, for example, in the late summer of 1916:

> For socialism is impossible without democracy because: (1) the proletariat cannot perform the socialist revolution unless it prepares for it by the struggle for democracy;
> (2) victorious socialism cannot consolidate its victory and bring humanity to the withering away of the state without implementing full democracy.[34]

But he had not forgotten the definition of 'dictatorship' he had worked out in 1906, and it remained his operative formula. 'Dictatorship,' he repeated, is a "domination of one part of society over the rest of society" that "rests directly on coercion."[35] And: "Dictatorship is state power based directly on *violence*."[36] His last reference before the March 1917 revolution came in a letter to Inessa Armand, emphasizing once again the connection with democracy: Armand should include the 'dictatorship of the proletariat' in a lecture to show

> why it is necessary, why it is impossible without arming the proletariat, why it is fully compatible with complete, all-round democracy (in spite of the vulgar opinion) . . .[37]

The interrevolution period—that is, the period from March to November 1917—can be considered, from our present narrow focus,

---

*For Lenin's identification of the "democratic republic" as the governmental form of the dictatorship of the proletariat, see the passage in a 1915 article: "The political form of a society wherein the proletariat is victorious in overthrowing the bourgeoisie will be a democratic republic . . . The abolition of classes is impossible without a dictatorship of the oppressed class, of the proletariat."[32]

the period in which *State and Revolution* was gestated.★ In this inter-revolution period there was a considerable uniformity about his references to the 'dictatorship of the proletariat,' and a notable characteristic was his full return to and repetition of the 1906 definition. For the first time in some years, the "no law" concept recurred, as he went back to his 1906 writing to answer the question: *What exactly is 'dictatorial' about the 'dictatorship of the proletariat'?* By April 1917 he was trying to define the proletarian half of the dual-power situation. The Soviet power, he said, constitutes a government alongside the government of the bourgeoisie, and—

> It is a revolutionary dictatorship, i.e., a power directly based on revolutionary seizure, on the direct initiative of the people from below, and *not on a law* enacted by a centralized state power.[38]

We see that Lenin has thrown in a new, ad-hoc qualifier, the last phrase about a "centralized" state power. Wasn't this power based on "law," authority, standards, rules, etc. established by a *non*centralized (or not-yet-centralized) state power? Lenin ignores this obvious question. He wants to emphasize the identity of the Soviet dual power with the Paris Commune, and will do so innumerable times in this period. But wasn't the power of the 1871 workers' state embodied in numerous *laws* and institutions established by the (nonparliamentary) representative assembly called the Commune? No answer. He simply repeats ever more emphatically:

> The fundamental characteristics of this type [of state power] are: (1) the source of power is not a law previously discussed and enacted by parliament, but the direct initiative of the people from below, in their local areas—direct "seizures" . . .

And he concludes: "This, and this *alone,* constitutes the *essence* of the Paris Commune as a special type of state."[39] What exactly is the "this alone" that constitutes its essence: that the "source of power" is "not a law"? (Untrue.) That it is nonparliamentary? (True.) That it is "local"? (Untrue.) That it is based on "direct initiative"? (Partly true.) That the "seizure" was "direct"? (Untrue.) Above all, that it was a workers' state? (True, but not mentioned by Lenin in this connection.) . . . I am

---

★The final draft appears to have been written in August–September, but Lenin had been studying the questions involved with special intensiveness since the last months of 1916, and indeed there was a draft already finished by July 1917.

trying to emphasize that several strands of thought were twisted into this statement.

This was only the first of several such passages that were now encountered in Lenin's writings, complicated further by the fact that the 'dictatorship' he kept defining was sometimes that of the proletariat and sometimes of the two-class variety. Not only was the "no law" definition back, and repeated more than once, but new characteristics were thrown in, with such apparent casualness that one wonders if he really thought they all meant the same thing.

Thus in May he specified that a 'dictatorship' "rests not on law, not on the formal will of the majority . . ."[40] By "formal will of the majority" he apparently meant elections; at any rate in June he made it explicit that the "scientific" meaning of 'dictatorship of the proletariat' meant "power based not on law or elections, but directly on the armed force of a particular section of the population."[41] But since the Soviets and the entire Soviet system were based on elections, what could this mean? And since he was specifically offering a definition, the power ceased to be a 'dictatorship' as soon as it *was* based on elections . . .

There was more to the muddle: in draft theses (which by nature were supposed to be worded with exactitude) one of the "Conclusions" was this:

> Bring home to the mass of workers, peasants and soldiers that the reason
> for the revolution's success locally is undivided power and the dic-
> tatorship of the proletariat.[42]

How on earth could the 'dictatorship of the proletariat'—which is the nationwide *outcome* of a revolutionary seizure of power—be the (prior) reason for success of the revolution *locally*? The least to be said about such usages is that they show how the phrase was taking on the character of a rubberized watchword, or code word, standing for something seen as a test of revolutionariness, but without a really scientific content.

These were the passages that preceded the final drafting of *State and Revolution.*

State and Revolution, which after all was the product of a more than one-year-long excogitation of the theory of the state, suggests that Lenin was rethinking his understanding of 'dictatorship' along with the rest of the subject. Conclusions cannot be too sweeping for two reasons: (1) The 'dictatorship of the proletariat' was not the question central to this work. The focus was on what Lenin called "smashing" the old state apparatus and inaugurating the process of "withering away" by a unique type of state (or nonstate). At no point did Lenin undertake a special exposition on 'dictatorship of the proletariat.' (2) The work was unfinished, stopping short of a chapter that was scheduled to discuss the lessons of 1905 and 1917. It is therefore risky to lean on what is *not* in the work.

Still, the first thing to be reported is that, after reviving the "no law" definition of 'dictatorship' all through the first part of 1917, Lenin failed to mention it once in *State and Revolution,* in connection with the numerous invocations of 'dictatorship of the proletariat.' He did mention a couple of elements associated with the definition: dictatorship was "undivided power directly backed by the armed force of the people."[43] In the midst of very strong emphases on the democracy of the 'dictatorship of the proletariat,' he did remark that it "imposes a series of restrictions on the freedom of the oppressors, the exploiters, the capitalists," indeed their "exclusion from democracy . . ."[44] This sentiment went all the way back to Plekhanov's views of 1903.

On the other hand, apart from these passing remarks, the content of the work brought overwhelmingly to the fore the conception of a new type of commune state that would open up democratic vistas. The 'dictatorship of the proletariat,' he stated strongly, was not a fixed formula, but would appear, during the transition period, in "a tremendous abundance and variety of political forms," just as the 'dictatorship of the bourgeoisie' did; and he denounced the social-democrats for claiming that "the 'dictatorship' of the proletariat 'contradicts' democracy!!"[45]

The most remarkable characteristic of *State and Revolution* was not directly associated with the 'dictatorship of the proletariat' references, but it was related to them. It was the emphasis in this work—and only here—on the *immediacy* of the 'withering away' pattern. Here is the prime text:

> The proletariat needs the state . . . But . . . according to Marx, the proletariat needs only a state which is withering away, i.e., a state so constituted that it begins to wither away immediately . . .[46]

A spotlight plays brightly on the unexpected last word. Let us look at a couple of related passages, for example at the little word 'soon' near the end of the following:

> Under socialism much of "primitive" democracy will inevitably be revived, since, for the first time in the history of civilized society, the *mass* of the population will rise to taking an *independent* part, not only in voting and elections, *but also in the everyday administration of the state.* Under socialism *all* will govern in turn and will soon become accustomed to no one governing.[47]

In another passage, there was no word like 'soon,' but its sense was implicit in the context: the suppression of a minority by a majority "is compatible with the extension of democracy to such an overwhelming majority of the population that the need for a *special machine* of suppression will begin to disappear."[48] The sense of immediacy was also applied *ex post facto* to the Paris Commune, which

> *was ceasing* to be a state since it had to suppress, not the majority of the population, but a minority (the exploiters) . . . And had the Commune become firmly established, all traces of the state in it would have "withered away" of themselves . . .[49]

Now of course it is especially this aspect of *State and Revolution* that has been scorned as utopian, as a momentary aberration on Lenin's part; but such skeptical remarks are partly based on misunderstanding. In the first place, "*begins* to wither away" should be read with great emphasis on the first word; it is a question above all of direction of development. In the second place, Lenin's thought was fixed specifically on the *suppressive* function of the state, its police side in the narrow sense.

But it is the suppressive function of a state that was regarded as its 'dictatorship' aspect; and so these remarks by Lenin in *State and Revolution* interest us hugely, even though they do not occur in passages discussing 'dictatorship.'

These were the ideas in Lenin's mind when the November revolution took place. From *State and Revolution* to November, there were only a couple of routine references to 'dictatorship,' one-class or two-class.[50] Right after the revolution, there was none. I wonder how long this would have lasted if the dissolution of the Constituent Assembly had not come up so soon. . . .

Lenin's first postrevolution mention of 'dictatorship of the proletariat' came in December in a statement, "Theses on the Constituent Assembly." The two references in this document were routine ones.[51] In January he dredged up and republished Plekhanov's advance justification, in 1903, of the suppression of the Assembly.[52]

5. The Steel Wire

Thus it began: the progressive subordination of the 'dictatorship of the proletariat' concept to the *immediate exigencies* of a Soviet state surrounded by counterrevolution, battered by White armies of intervention, ruined industrially, starved by the imperialist blockade, struggling to stay alive until revolution in the West could come to the aid of the beleaguered fortress.

This is the real history; our own subject lies in one small corner of it. There were legions of casualties; individuals, institutions, and ideas were equally done to death. The pressures were gigantic; and mere concepts were crushed out of shape. All this requires a different history from this one.

But before we go to the small corner, let us note two things about the larger picture.

(1) During the period when the revolution was fighting for life against fourteen invading armies, Lenin thought that the outcome was going to be *either/or:* either the military overthrow of the Russian Revolution before the European Revolution could save it, or else the expansion of the revolution into a Continental and worldwide upheaval—the final destruction of capitalism over the entire planet. He did not count on the in-between situation that actually took place: a level of European revolution and of war exhaustion sufficient to blunt the imperialist world's intervention *without* bringing about a social revolution on the Continent, so that the Russian Revolution survived *militarily*—but isolated. The Beleaguered Fortress had been waiting for the revolutionary war to be won, so that it would be relieved. Now the war was over; and the fortress was still beleaguered.

All Russian Marxists had for decades explained that in their country a purely proletarian government, a socialist government, would be unviable, short of world revolution. That meant: a counterrevolutionary overthrow was inevitable. It would seem, therefore, unnecessary to explain why the universally expected actually happened—except for one detail. The counterrevolution came from *inside* the ruling party, which was not overthrown but which, rather, overthrew the workers' state. If this were a different history, we would have to explain this, and account for the fact that the beleaguered workers' state established by the Bolshevik party was transformed into a state ruled by the collective bureaucracy: the internal counterrevolution called Stalinism.

But, as we said, that is a different story, and what we have to highlight is simply this: a counterrevolution *had* to take place inside the Beleaguered Fortress, *and it did*—whatever you think the counterrevolution was.

(2) Such a counterrevolution, as we have already stressed, was the outcome of enormous sociopolitical pressures; and one of the consequences of pressure is that it deforms. Inside the Beleaguered Fortress, principles and concepts came under deforming pressure too. Stress produces temporary distortions: if you hang a series of weights on a steel wire, the wire will stretch—and stretch again—until the weights are removed, after which the wire snaps back to its original size. In physics, it is said that the strain on the wire did not exceed the steel's elastic limit. In politics, it is said that the deformation was not outside the bounds of principle.

In one of the alternate-time universes well known to science-fiction readers, perhaps the German Revolution of 1918–1920 burst through the bonds imposed by the Social-Democrats, and Soviet Germany came into existence, with its economic efficiency, educated and advanced proletariat, technical knowledge and wealth. Germany plus Russia equals Communist Europe, Lenin said. Soviet Russia became a rather dreary backwater of the new world, carried along on the élan of the European Revolution. The steel wire in the Beleaguered Fortress had stretched and stretched, and now could snap back to its original length . . .

But since this did not happen in our universe, let us define what actually did take place. If we interpret the steel-wire metaphor of elasticity, what happened was this: under the intolerable pressures of isolation in the Beleaguered Fortress, principles were first distorted by the strain of emergency exceptions, and *then the distortions themselves became the principles.*

The steel wire stands for workers' and party democracy. This pattern was acted out with reference to a number of questions having to do with the capacity of the new Soviet institutions to facilitate control from below. A typical question of this sort was that of the decision of the Tenth Party Congress in 1921 to abolish organized factions—a decision which Trotsky later agreed helped lay the *juridical* basis for Stalin's despotic regime. It was typical because it was proposed and adopted as an emergency exception, a deviation from the desirable degree of democracy, justified only by the life-and-death needs of the moment; and having been adopted for this reason, it became accepted as the *norm*. The question of a one-party state went through a similar evolution.

Wherever you look into Soviet politics during this period, you see "exceptions" turning into norms. The steel wire was refusing to snap back; it had stretched, and stayed stretched. This was the molecular process of internal degeneration.

If every concept and institution of workers' democracy was under strain in the Beleaguered Fortress, the concept of the 'dictatorship of the proletariat' and of 'dictatorship' in general was under the hammer. It is only a question of tracing how, by whom, and how rapidly distortions were turning into norms. The question of tempo was crucial, for no one could know at the time how soon the Beleaguered Fortress would be relieved.

In this period there is no point in simply listing mentions of the 'dictatorship' concept; it is a question of finding the points where new strains were put on the steel wire.

6. 'Dictatorship' in Year One

We are, then, looking into that small corner of the history of this period which is under the sign of the 'dictatorship of the proletariat.' The first ominous incident to record was an expulsion, a proceeding that used to be rare in the party. This involved the expulsion from the Bolshevik party of its trade-union leader, A. Lozovsky. According to Lenin's draft resolution of January 1918, he had to be expelled for holding *opinions:*

> . . . he expressed opinions which radically diverge from those of the Party and of the revolutionary proletariat in general, but coincide on all major points with the petty-bourgeois negation of the dictatorship of the proletariat . . .

Lozovsky had to be expelled because he "does not understand the necessity for the dictatorship of the proletariat . . . which sticks at no bourgeois–democratic formulas . . ." But this was careless, unbuttoned language: he was not being expelled for a lack of "understanding." Point 6 was more enlightening: party membership was impossible for one who refuses to accept the idea that it is the duty of the trade unions to take upon themselves state functions . . .[53]

Here the 'dictatorship of the proletariat' was made the ideological ground of the expulsion—for the first time, I believe. Even worse was the real reason: Lozovsky had refused, as head of the trade unions, to go along with the Central Committee's perspective of integrating the trade unions into the state machinery.* Later Lenin himself approached this same position, in the so-called Trade-Union Controversy of 1920; Lozovsky was later readmitted to the party; but a considerable weight had been hung on the steel wire.

In an unpublished piece of the same month, Lenin remarked: "What dictatorship implies and means is a state of simmering war, a state of military measures of struggle against the enemies of the proletariat in power."[55] For a formula that sounds like a definition, the insertion of "*military* measures" indicated to what extent the special characteristics of the period were blurring in Lenin's mind with what, on the next page, he called the "scientific" term for breaking capitalist resistance.

Toward the end of the month came a speech—made to the Third All-Russia Congress of Soviets on January 25—that we can qualify, like certain predecessors, as a theoretical disaster. Perhaps he was short of sleep that day. . . but, for whatever reason, *this* is what came out:

> One of the objectors [on the Right] declared that we had favored the dictatorship of democracy, that we had recognized the rule of democracy. That declaration was so absurd, so utterly meaningless, that it is merely a collection of words. It is just like saying "iron snow," or something similar. . . .
>
> Those who talk so much about the dictatorship of democracy merely utter meaningless, absurd phrases which indicate neither economic knowledge nor political understanding.[56]

"One of the objectors" may have been a representative of the Left S.R.'s, who around this time were raising the watchword of the "dictatorship of democracy" (or of "the Democracy") instead of 'dictatorship of the proletariat,' meaning the "dictatorship" of the peasantry along with the proletariat; so says O. H. Radkey.[57]

Could Lenin really not remember ever hearing talk of the "dic-

---

*A year later, the teachers' union congress heard from Lenin that "only those unions which recognize the revolutionary class struggle for socialism by the dictatorship of the proletariat can be full and equal members of the trade unions."[54]

tatorship of [the] democracy"? Didn't it at least remind him of a certain famous formula called the "democratic dictatorship"? He not only reiterated this claim of complete meaninglessness, without offering any explanation, but in addition launched the following attack on "democracy," *tout court:*

> Democracy is a form of bourgeois state championed by all traitors to genuine socialism . . . who assert that democracy is contrary to the dictatorship of the proletariat. Until the revolution transcended the limits of the bourgeois system, we were for democracy; but as soon as we saw the first signs of socialism in the progress of the revolution, we took a firm and resolute stand for the dictatorship of the proletariat.

It would be hard to be more vulgar in flatly counterposing "democracy" to "dictatorship" in abstract terms—exactly what he had warned against more than once. The extreme theoretical ineptness of this passage is hard to understand, but its political import is not, especially given the current of the times.

This may have been pointed out to Lenin at the time; for the next day, at a Railway Union congress, he spoke very differently: "it is not true that we are destroying democracy," etc., and he lauded the Soviets as a higher form of democracy, a "real democracy," and so on.[58] But a couple of months later, the "correction" was in turn forgotten: the alternatives, he said, were either the dictatorship of the proletariat or "the dictatorship of the bourgeoisie, disguised by . . . democracy and similar bourgeois frauds . . ."[59] (We will come back to this question in Chapter 5, Section 7.)

In the spring, the word 'iron' began appearing in his descriptions of the 'dictatorship of the proletariat.'[60] This proved metallurgically that he could not have been talking about a class dictatorship. "Either the dictatorship of Kornilov . . . or the dictatorship of the proletariat," he asserted;[61] but "Kornilov" was not a social class. At the same time the 'dictatorship of the proletariat' concept began sounding like an all-purpose fix-it man:

> . . . our dictatorship of the proletariat is the establishment of order, discipline, labor, productivity, accounting and control by the proletarian Soviet power . . .[62]

Perhaps it made good coffee too? It was customary to proclaim that the 'dictatorship' had to crush the "exploiters," but then Lenin threw in: "exploiters and hooligans . . ."[63] The idea of a *class* dictatorship directed against "hooligans" boggles the mind. The invocation of "dictatorial methods" also began looking like a cure-all:

> . . . our task is to study the state capitalism of the Germans, to spare *no effort* in copying it and not shrink from adopting *dictatorial* methods to hasten the copying of it.[64]

This referred to the German war economy, involving coercion of the capitalist class, i.e., suggesting a state "dictatorship" over the ruling class. By an unstated chain of thought, this passage ended with an appeal not to "hesitate to use barbarous methods in fighting barbarism." Again: obviously the 'dictatorship of the proletariat' was not merely a class concept when he urged that "there must be a dictatorship throughout the whole of Russia" and "not only centrally."[65]

At the end of Year One, Lenin spoke at an anniversary meeting where he sought to summarize the year:

> . . . this past year has been one of genuine proletarian dictatorship. This concept used to be mysterious book Latin, a mouthful of incomprehensible words. [Like 'revolutionary-democratic dictatorship of the proletariat and the peasantry'?] Intellectuals sought an explanation of the concept in learned works, which only gave them a hazy notion of what the proletarian dictatorship was all about.

The only such learned work in existence was his own *State and Revolution*. This philistine passage continued as follows:

> The chief thing that stands to our credit during this past year is that we have translated these words from abstruse Latin into plain Russian. During this past year the working class has not been engaged in idle philosophizing, but in the practical work of creating and exercising a proletarian dictatorship . . .[66]

The process of translation into "plain Russian" was that of burying the *class* meaning of the 'dictatorship of the proletariat' under its police aspect. The next day, on November 7, he spoke to an anniversary rally of the Cheka staff, and told them: "The important thing for us is that Cheka is directly exercising the dictatorship of the proletariat . . ."[67] Presumably the rest of the state was exercising it only indirectly.

By the end of Year One, it was clear that Lenin was no longer using 'dictatorship of the proletariat' to denote a workers' state that was subject to the democratic rule of the working classes. It now meant a specially organized dictatorial regime, dictatorial in the sense that had become increasingly dominant, and increasingly counterposed to abstract democracy. We will see in the next chapter that a number of Bolshevik spokesmen carried this process of theoretical degeneration even further, thus facilitating (though certainly not causing) the societal counterrevolution represented by Stalin.

5
The International Debate on 'Dictatorship'

In tracing a mere phrase, even one so influential as 'dictatorship of the proletariat,' through the history of the socialist movement, we not only face the danger of missing the forest for the trees, but in fact we have to succumb to the danger: for there is simply no room on these pages for the whole "forest." In this case, the "forest" is the fact that, from 1917 into the early 1920s, a world revolution swept over most of Europe.

Several decades of historians have worked hard to expunge even mention of the First World Revolution from the books, so that literate people can read whole volumes on postwar history without necessarily learning that such a revolution took place. In fact, the dominant circles of academic historiography have virtually dropped the First World Revolution of 1917–1921/22 down the Memory Hole. But at this point we cannot ignore it.

1. The European Upheaval

The First World Revolution, starting with Russia, flamed out most violently over Eastern Europe, Hungary, Austria, Germany, and Italy, with shocks and aftershocks in other parts of Europe and reverberations in the rest of the world. In all of these countries there were two leading watchwords, or "slogans," derived from the Russian Revolution, not through the machinations of agitators but mainly through the headlines in the world press. One of these had to do with 'soviets,' whether this term was left in its Russian form (as in *"Les soviets partout!"*) or translated (as into German, *Räte*). The other slogan was the 'dictatorship of the proletariat,' which the world was told had been established in Russia, and was accordingly denounced or cheered.

Along with some form of the slogan "All power to the Councils!" the cry of "Dictatorship of the proletariat" literally became a watchword of the day among millions of European workers—for the first and last time in history. During Year One and increasingly after it, the term 'dictatorship of the proletariat' first became a routine journalistic designation for the Soviet Russian regime, a commonplace label, as the press echoed the Bolsheviks' own usage, even if pejoratively. Since Lenin and his followers insisted that they had it straight from Marx, countless Authorities repeated the claim, all the more gladly if Marx could be smeared with the alleged crimes being committed in Moscow. This part of the story has a great deal of sociological interest, but is not relevant to our present concerns.

More important: these two phrases, having been trumpeted around the world through various channels, were also adopted by the revolutionary left, Communist or non-Communist, in several revolutionary situations. Take Italy . . .

Italy was overwhelmingly peasant, but revolutionary feeling penetrated it deeply in the immediate postwar period. Don Sturzo, the Catholic priest who headed the Partito Popolare in the center of Italian politics between left and right, later wrote about the mass appeal of the cry *'Viva Lenin!'*—a phrase that acted as a précis of the two slogans.

> The laboring classes had been neutralist during the war. Now, through economic sufferings and political crisis, they turned against those who had willed the war and, at the same time, against the middle classes [i.e., the bourgeoisie], lending a willing ear to the socialists who extolled the dictatorship of the proletariat.[1]

Pietro Nenni, the future leader of Italian socialism, also related that "Then the peasant, like the workingman in the towns, gave utterance to the cry of 'Long live Lenin!' "[2] Sturzo casually referred to the Socialists' advocacy of "an economic dictatorship of the proletariat in Italy," by which he meant a set of collectivist measures:[3]

> It was the time when, to quote Serrati, the discussion of every question was flavored with the dictatorship of the proletariat.[4]

Serrati was the postwar leader of the Socialist Party, which at its congress in October 1919 adopted a new, revolutionary programmatic statement which asserted that "nothing but the dictatorship of the proletariat could bring about the disappearance of class distinctions and thereby the establishment of Socialism."[5]

Or take France . . .

The political temperature can be gauged from the fact that in 1919–20 Léon Blum embraced the 'dictatorship of the proletariat' as whole-heartedly as the next reformist. And it did not make too much difference to him if it was the dictatorship of a party or a class. In 1919 he declared that French history proves that a revolutionary regime cannot rely on the institutions it has overthrown:

> All the political revolutions of the nineteenth century . . . have failed or succeeded depending on whether or not they took the precaution of bringing about the construction and legal installation of the new regime: this intermediate period of dictatorship, which when it involves the social revolution is the impersonal dictatorship of the proletariat but which has been or would have been, in other epochs and vis-à-vis other revolutions, the dictatorship of the royalist party, Bonapartist party or republican party.

When bourgeois hypocrites condemn "the idea of the dictatorship of the proletariat," he said, they deny revolutionary and republican justice.[6]

At the split Congress of Tours in 1920, Blum protested that he was a partisan of the dictatorship of the proletariat, afraid "of neither the word nor the thing."[7] A biography relates that he

> accepted the dictatorship of a party or of a class. He rejected the dictatorship of a handful of known or unknown partisans. Nor would he have anything to do with a dictatorship that would outlast the crisis and would grow into a system of government.[8]

It is clear that Blum thought of the 'dictatorship of the proletariat' as a suspension of democratic norms.

Or take Austria . . .

Otto Bauer was one of the top leaders of the Austrian Social-Democracy at this point in history, when the party was working hard to prevent a socialist revolution, and he wrote a detailed description of how this effort was carried out: his book *The Austrian Revolution*. He can, then, be believed when he describes what he and his colleagues were up against, after the formation of the new socialist-led armed force, the *Volkswehr:*

> Wild excitement prevailed in the barracks of the *Volkswehr* . . . In the discussions within the Soldiers' Councils Social Democrats and Commu-

nists fought out their hardest battles . . . Every edition of the newspaper brought news of the struggles of Spartacus in Germany. Every speech announced the glory of the great Russian Revolution, which with one stroke had abolished exploitation forever. The masses, who had just seen the overthrow of the once so powerful Empire, recked nothing of the strength of Entente capitalism; they believed that the Revolution would now wing its way to the victorious countries. "Dictatorship of the proletariat." "All power to the councils." These were the cries that now resounded through the streets.[9]

It did not enter Bauer's head, either while he was engaged in putting the revolution to sleep or later when he was writing about it, to claim that the 'dictatorship of the proletariat' would be an offense against the democratic will of the people; on the contrary, the Austrian proletariat "considered the establishment of the dictatorship of the proletariat to be possible." The overwhelming argument with which the "excited" masses were lulled into quiescence was the cry that proletarian power would so offend the Allied conquerors, who had just made the world safe for democracy, that they would step in to smash the new Austrian democracy and kill the revolution plus as many people as got in their way. "The dictatorship of the proletariat," summed up Bauer, "would have ended with the dictatorship of foreign commanders."[10] At the same time that the German Social-Democrats were explaining that the dictatorship of the proletariat had to be rejected in favor of the greater democracy of bourgeois democracy, their Austrian comrades argued that the dictatorship of the proletariat had to be given up because the bourgeois-democrats would impose a military dictatorship.

That argument ended the matter, as far as this Austro-Marxist theoretician was concerned. What has to be stressed is that the argument was not over "dictatorship"—it was over *revolution*. Indeed, the 'dictatorship of the proletariat' was seen as the rule of socialist democracy: take the German Independents . . .

2. Germany: The Twin Slogans

In Germany, where the Social-Democratic Party had split during the war, the left-wing Independent Social-Democratic Party (ISDP)★

★Here I use party initials based on the English-language form of the party name: for example, the Social-Democratic Party is abbreviated 'SDP.' In German, and in many adopted the 'dictatorship of the proletariat' into its program. Before the German Revolution of November 1918, only the Spartacus League wing of the Independents had called for "workers' and soldiers' councils and a socialist dictatorship of the proletariat."[11] Afterwards, this programmatic watchword was taken up by the left wing of the ISDP (Däumig, Richard Müller, Ledebour); and in short order—such was the pressure of revolutionary feeling—even by the rest of the party leadership (Haase et al.). But it did not mean the same thing to all of these elements.

Däumig wrote, early in 1919: "In the council system we shall first prepare the dictatorship of the proletariat organically. With it we shall secondly conquer political power and thirdly, after the victory, carry through the dictatorship of the proletariat in the economic process as well as in the machinery of state." At the ISDP congress in March 1919,

> Däumig found the two terms, council system and dictatorship of the proletariat, "synonymous"; and the dictatorship was thus invested with all the radical democratic idealism of the council idea itself.[12]

Under pressure, the party's right-wingers were willing to include the two watchwords in the program, but they wanted insurance. The congress program added a phrase in apposition: ". . . the dictatorship of the proletariat, the representative of the great majority of the people . . . ," and also appended a sentence: "Only socialism brings the elimination of class rule, the elimination of any dictatorship, true democracy."[13] On means, the program added: "To reach this goal [socialism], the [ISDP] employs all political and economic means of struggle, *including parliaments.*"[14] (Emphasis in original.)

All of this compromise language, which Däumig opposed, was in code: the point was to suggest that the 'dictatorship of the proletariat' would be exercised through *parliamentary* forms, and that only parliamentary forms could determine a legitimate majority. This perspective was concretized by the proposal to inter the council system in the constitution as an adjunct to the parliamentary structure that was

---

historical works in English, the name *Sozialdemokratische Partei Deutschlands* is abbreviated 'SPD.' The two usages carry over to the Independents: *Unabhängige Sozialdemokratische Partei Deutschlands* was abbreviated 'USPD' in German; but here I use the English form 'ISDP.'

envisioned. When the revolutionary situation died down, this "compromise" was naturally swept into the dustbin; in the meantime it performed its function of confusing the issue of the revolution (class power) sufficiently to split the inexperienced left.

Hence for a while the twin watchwords—council system and dictatorship of the proletariat—seemed to gain general acceptance as far right as the center of the Majority Social-Democratic Party:

> The idea of workers' councils in some form [writes historian D. W. Morgan] was held by a broad section of the socialist movement, not only by Communists and radical Independents but also by most moderate Independents, much of the Majority Socialist rank and file, and even a few leading members of the SPD [Majority S-D Party].[15]

"Everybody" was for the councils (Räte, soviets). In his eyewitness account of revolutionary Europe in 1919, *Across the Blockade,* H. N. Brailsford reported that the "Weimar" idea (that is, parliamentarism) was held in general contempt. "An ever widening circle saw in the Workers' and Soldiers' Councils, based on the Russian Soviet model, the future structure of representation in Germany." Even aside from the left, "the more moderate parties were obliged to fall into step."[16] While he was in Berlin, "continual declarations of adhesions to some form of the Council idea were appearing in the press"—for example, from the well-known liberal economist Professor Lujo Brentano, and also from the employers' organization in Berlin.[17]

The 'council' slogan could be, and was, embraced by the antirevolutionary right wing of the Social-Democrats—embraced and squeezed out of shape; but the 'dictatorship of the proletariat' watchword, accompanying it, reached a sticking point. This was dramatized out when the counterrevolution launched the Kapp putsch in March 1920, so that there was an immediate question of cooperation between the two socialist parties to organize the answering general strike. The ISDP agreed to act together with the Majority S-D Party on a number of conditions, one of which stated that "the goal of the dictatorship of the proletariat must be acknowledged." This was a shorthand (or coded) way of saying: the German proletariat will mobilize to defend this government only if its sacrifices and struggle will be repaid with the declaration of a workers' socialist republic and not merely a return to the capitalist *status quo ante.* The Social-Democrats boggled at *this* condition alone, and thus it was determined that there would be two separate strike commands instead of a unified one. Even in the face of possible disaster the Social-Democrats refused to abandon the maintenance of capitalism during the revolutionary situation.[18]

Not that the Social-Democrats claimed a socialist republic was contrary to the people's wishes. "Everybody" was for "socialism." Even the Democratic Party, the party of bourgeois liberalism, came out for "socialism" in its program.[19] When, on the morrow of the November revolution, the Independents posed their conditions for an all-socialist coalition government, their first demand was for a "Socialist republic." The Majority Social-Democrats agreed—only it had to wait for a Constituent Assembly (while in the meantime capitalism was put back on its feet).

When the Independents demanded that all state power be in the hands of "chosen men of the total laboring population and the soldiers," the Social-Democrats replied: "If this demand means the dictatorship of a part, a class, without the majority behind it, we must reject this demand because it would run counter to our democratic principles."[20] But their democratic principles had not prevented them from proclaiming the end of the monarchy and the Empire, from a balcony, on their own say-so, without so much as a vote by their own cabinet. Their democratic principles would allow them to do much— for example, to make secret pacts with counterrevolutionary generals—but these principles always brought them up short when it was a question of touching the capitalist system.

In short: while there *was* an issue about 'dictatorship,' the issue for the ruling Social-Democrats was not 'dictatorship' but socialist revolution. The 'dictatorship of the proletariat' meant, to the Independent left as to Luxemburg, nothing more dictatorial than the establishment of a socialist republic on the basis of the existing Workers' and Soldiers' Councils; what the majority Social-Democrats counterposed to this state order was parliament—but a parliament that did not yet exist, that was supposed to come into existence in the future. *In the meantime, what was the democratic basis of the Social-Democratic government, which was so steadfastly insisting on restoring capitalism?*

By its own lights: nothing. This government of alleged principled democrats was self-appointed, mob-installed; they had simply seized the power as it rolled in the street. The sole legitimation of this government came when it convinced a certain representative assembly to acknowledge its power; and this assembly was that of the same

Workers' and Soldiers' Councils whose power it condemned as undemocratic.

The only 'dictatorship'—in the accurate historical sense—was at this point being wielded by the Majority Social-Democratic ministers themselves, who had never been elected by anyone, who had appointed themselves as starkly as any other dictator: the same Social-Democratic ministers who in the name of democracy were piously denouncing the 'dictatorship' of the revolutionary representative assembly of workers and soldiers.

When the revolutionary pressure eased off, when the red wave was damping down, the practical-minded parliamentarians set about constructing, on the ashes of the German Revolution, a new bourgeois republic that was guaranteed to be unviable, indeed impractical.

The 'dictatorship of the proletariat,' derived from the formulations of the German Independents and the Russian left Mensheviks (Martov, etc.), was also incorporated into the program of the so-called Two-and-a-Half International or Vienna Union (properly named the International Working Union of Socialist Parties), which existed from February 1921 to May 1923.[21]

3. View from the Left: Rosa Luxemburg

At the moment of the German Revolution, that is, in November 1918, the Independent Social-Democratic Party enjoyed the membership of the leading figures of all three wings—left, right, and center—of the prewar Social-Democratic Party. On the extreme right, there was the father of Revisionism, Eduard Bernstein, whose pacifistic Anglophilia had turned him against the social-imperialist Majority faction; in the so-called "Marxist center" was the papal figure of Karl Kautsky; and as for the leading theoretician of the Marxist left, Rosa Luxemburg, her Spartacus League was still affiliated with the Independents. At the end of December 1918 the Spartacists established the Communist Party as a separate organization; around the same time Bernstein rejoined the Majority S-D Party without relinquishing membership in the ISDP (until the latter outlawed dual membership in March); but Kautsky stayed in the ISDP until its rump, rejecting unity with the CP, merged back into the Social-Democratic Party in 1922.

We have seen what a considerable public role was played during this period by the 'dictatorship of the proletariat' slogan in association with the 'councils' or 'soviet' concept. One would expect that socialist theoreticians would confront the problem of analyzing what these ideas meant. To what extent was this expectation realized? This is the subject of this section and the next two sections.

Luxemburg's reaction to the problem was first and foremost directed to the Russian situation. She was in jail in Germany up to the November revolution, which released her; hence during Year One of the Russian Revolution she was able to get only incomplete information on what was going on. This must be kept in mind while reading her essay on "The Russian Revolution," written under these circumstances and left unfinished.

Time is partially suspended during the enforced stasis of prison life; Luxemburg was shielded, or buffered, not so much from the impact of the Bolshevik revolution itself as from the impact of its reception in the movement. She came out of jail exactly the same revolutionary that had gone in; it was the others who were changed a little by events. And the views she expressed in this manuscript were exactly the same as those recounted in Chapter 2; but they were now applied to Soviet Russia.

Luxemburg made fairly frequent use of the term 'dictatorship of the proletariat' in this essay, as everyone else was doing. On this issue, as on others, her tone was generally that of sympathetic, friendly warning to the Russian leaders. Everyone with 20/20 hindsight, of course, knows that her warnings were largely vindicated.

She reminded the reader that this was "the very first experiment in proletarian dictatorship in world history" (ignoring the Paris Commune), and so it would be "crazy" to expect everything to be done perfectly. The real alternatives were the "victory of the counterrevolution or dictatorship of the proletariat—Kaledin or Lenin." The Bolsheviks were right to set their goal not as "the safeguarding of bourgeois democracy, but a dictatorship of the proletariat for the purpose of realizing socialism."[22]

But she criticized Lenin's apparent view that the dictatorship of the proletariat entailed the disfranchisement of nonworkers on a permanent basis, supportable as such measures were in the first period of consolidation.* It is "not a necessity of dictatorship," she said.[25]

---

*Lenin's pronouncements had given this impression to friends and foes alike. A little

The Bolsheviks are wrong to think that there is "a ready-made formula" for the socialist transformation and the dictatorship of the proletariat; what is most essential is the political education of the masses. "Decree, dictatorial force of the factory overseer, draconic penalties, rule by terror—all these things are but palliatives."[26] If political life is repressed, if elections are eliminated and freedoms restricted, "public life gradually falls asleep," and the regime becomes a "clique affair—a dictatorship, to be sure, not the dictatorship of the proletariat, however, but only the dictatorship of a handful of politicians, that is a dictatorship in the bourgeois sense, in the sense of the rule of the Jacobins . . ."[27]

Above all, she pounced on some of the fundamental errors involved in Lenin's rationale for the dictatorship that was actually being erected: for one thing, this rationale was the social-democrats' theory turned inside-out.

> The basic error of the Lenin-Trotsky theory is that they too, just like Kautsky, oppose dictatorship to democracy. "Dictatorship *or* democracy" is the way the question is put by Bolsheviks and Kautsky alike. The latter naturally decides in favor of "democracy," that is, of bourgeois democracy, precisely because he opposes it to the alternative of the socialist revolution. Lenin and Trotsky, on the other hand, decide in favor of dictatorship in contradistinction to democracy, and thereby in favor of the dictatorship of a handful of persons, that is, in favor of dictatorship on the bourgeois model. They are two opposite poles, both alike being far removed from a genuine socialist policy. The proletariat . . . should and must at once undertake socialist measures in the most energetic, unyielding and unhesitant fashion, in other words, exercise a dictatorship but a dictatorship of the *class,* not of a party or of a clique— dictatorship of the class, that means in the broadest public form on the basis of the most active, unlimited participation of the mass of people, of unlimited democracy.[28]

---

later, in the course of the international debate, no doubt after thinking the question over, Lenin agreed that disfranchisement was a special measure. For example, he told the Eighth Party Congress in March 1919:

> We do not at all regard the question of disfranchising the bourgeoisie from an absolute point of view, because it is theoretically quite conceivable that the dictatorship of the proletariat may suppress the bourgeoisie at every step without disfranchising them. . . . Nor do we propose our Constitution as a model for other countries. . . . while it is essential to suppress the bourgeoisie as a class, it is not essential to deprive them of suffrage and of equality."[23]

He had devoted a substantial section to this point in his *Proletarian Revolution and the Renegade Kautsky.*[24]

She did not simply reiterate that 'proletarian dictatorship' equaled 'proletarian democracy'; she explained what the relationship was:

> But socialist democracy is not something which begins only in the promised land after the foundations of socialist economy are created; it does not come as some sort of Christmas present for the worthy people who, in the interim, have loyally supported a handful of socialist dictators. Socialist democracy begins simultaneously with the beginnings of the destruction of class rule and of the construction of socialism. It begins at the very moment of the seizure of power by the socialist party. It is the same thing as the dictatorship of the proletariat.
>
> Yes, dictatorship! But this dictatorship consists in the *manner of applying democracy,* not in its elimination; in energetic, resolute attacks upon the well-entrenched rights and economic relationships of bourgeois society, without which a socialist transformation cannot be accomplished. But this dictatorship must be the work of the *class* and not of a little leading minority in the name of the class . . .[29]

If we consider the difficulties under which she was viewing the events, we must agree that it took a flash of insight for her to put forward an idea that was so simple it was hard to see: the idea that the Bolsheviks were falling into the fatal trap of turning exceptions into norms. She was ready to go along with emergency measures taken in the life-and-death struggle going on as the Soviet government fought against the intervention; she would not cry havoc just because mistakes were made; for the danger began elsewhere:

> It would be demanding something superhuman from Lenin and his comrades if we should expect of them that under such circumstances they should conjure forth the finest democracy, the most exemplary dictatorship of the proletariat and a flourishing socialist economy. . . . The danger begins only when they make a virtue of necessity and want to freeze into a complete theoretical system all the tactics forced upon them by these fatal circumstances, and want to recommend them to the international proletariat as a model of socialist tactics.[30]

And, finally, she had an opinion on who was mainly responsible for the undesirable excesses in Russia. They were the people who were responsible for the *isolation* of the Russian workers' state: the German Social-Democrats who yesterday had been kaiser-socialists and now were propping up capitalism at home, keeping the German socialist revolution chloroformed.

Let the German Government Socialists cry that the rule of the Bolsheviks in Russia is a distorted expression of the dictatorship of the proletariat. If it was or is such, that is only because it is a product of the behavior of the German proletariat itself, in itself a distorted expression of the socialist class struggle.[31]

The Bolsheviks' great service was that they were the only ones who could say *"I have dared!"* (Hutten's immortal cry). "In Russia the problem could only be posed. It could not be solved in Russia. And in *this* sense, the future everywhere belongs to 'Bolshevism.'"[32]

Luxemburg's writings, from the time she was freed by the revolution up to her murder in January 1919, showed the political-publicist use she made of the 'dictatorship of the proletariat' as a popular watchword—a watchword resounding in the streets, colored by all the hopes felt for the Russian Revolution by German revolutionary workers. An examination of how she treated it, especially in *Die Rote Fahne* (which succeeded *Spartacus* on the founding of the Communist Party), shows how she filled it with democratic content, not merely in terms of theoretical exposition but also in political agitation. For example:

It is not a question today of democracy or dictatorship. The question placed on the order of the day by history reads: *bourgeois* democracy or *socialist* democracy. For dictatorship of the proletariat is democracy in the socialist sense. Dictatorship of the proletariat does not mean bombs, putsches, riots, "anarchy," as the agents of capitalist profit deliberately lie, but it is the utilization of all political means of power to realize socialism and expropriate the capitalist class—in accordance with the revolutionary majority of the proletariat and by its will, hence in the spirit of socialist democracy.[33]

Such an armament of the compact working masses of the people with the whole of the political power for the tasks of the revolution—this is the dictatorship of the proletariat and therefore real democracy.[34]

The entire German press, she declared, from the conservative-right *Kreuz-Zeitung* to the Social-Democratic *Vorwärts*, "resounds with denunciations of 'terror,' 'putschism,' 'anarchy,' 'dictatorship.'" The same people who for four years of war turned Europe into a pile of ruins now cry 'anarchy' against the proletarian dictatorship; the same people who presided over "the greatest bloodbath ever seen" now raucously chorus over the alleged "terror" that is threatened by the dictatorship of the proletariat. The truth is that it is the bourgeoisie that launches real anarchy and makes real putsches whenever it finds it needful, "to smother the proletarian revolution, to make the socialist dictatorship fall in chaos, and on the ruins of the revolution erect the class dictatorship of capital forever."[35]

Our programmatic goal, she told the Independents, must be "to establish the political rule of the great mass of workingpeople, the dictatorship of the workers' and soldiers' councils."[36]

In these articles—which were of course part of the political campaign pursued by the entire Spartacist group—we see what was probably the one and only agitational campaign by a revolutionary Marxist based on the 'dictatorship of the proletariat' concept in Marx's sense.

Luxemburg's use of the term was, as we have seen, not typical; indeed it was unique. It should be ranged alongside the case of another leftist leader of the Independents, Emil Barth.

Barth was one of the leaders of the Metal Workers Union and of the Revolutionary Shop Stewards group led by Richard Müller. The government moved to put Müller out of action by drafting him into the army; Müller proposed Barth as his replacement; and on February 9, 1918, a meeting of the opposition group met to elect Barth. But first Barth had to make a stridently "revolutionary" speech (according to his own memoirs) to state the "conditions" under which he accepted the post. The chief condition was the committee's adoption of a "revolutionary aim":

> The aim [he said] is a proletarian peace, i.e., a peace forced through by the proletariat; that is, socialism; that is, the dictatorship of the proletariat.

This formulation is so awkward that one has a right to suspect what this inveterate "self-dramatizer" meant by the phrase, which he thus picked out of the air. First of all he tied it up with the traditional rationale for a Jacobin-Communist dictatorship, viz., the corruption of the body politic.[37]

> Patriotism [orated Barth] has manured Europe with blood, with human blood and bodies; its pestilential miasma has poisoned souls; the very breath of the people, of mountains, valleys, fields and forests is greed and cruelty. Everything, everything is poisoned . . . Into this maelstrom of avarice and rottenness almost everything has been drawn. [And so on.]

True, Barth did not specifically draw the conclusion that this sad condition made it impossible for the people to emancipate *themselves*.

Instead, he drew a different positive conclusion: the need for organization—dictatorial organization.

> Organization forms the backbone of everything and has to be worked out as follows:
> At the top, a dictator, with unlimited powers. Everyone has to submit to his orders or instructions. Everyone has to carry out what he is directed to do, without asking why or wherefore. Only those who stand at the top have the right to hand out tasks, so that everything that takes place is done in a unified way.

This was clear enough, but Barth added that "bourgeois morality" had to be shelved for the nonce. Then he huffed-and-puffed to a closing threat that "death" would be the penalty for "betraying" the illegal opposition movement. There was no ambiguity about the identity of the unlimited dictator.[38]

(About a year later, this same Barth was one of the three Independent coalition ministers cohabiting in the cabinet with the Majority Social-Democrats and denouncing Karl Liebknecht as a revolutionary fanatic.)

What Barth understood by 'dictatorship of the proletariat' was perfectly plain: abandonment of democratic rights and practices in favor of dictatorial forms of government. Just as plain was the source from which he had absorbed this conception. For, unlike the other figures highlighted in this chapter, Barth's background was not Marxist, but anti-Marxist; up to 1911, when he became active in the Metal Workers Union, he had been an active anarchist.[39]

Within the left, the significant counterposition is: Luxemburg versus Barth.

4. Views from the Right

In Luxemburg's writings of 1918 we have seen one revolutionary Marxist interpretation of the newly enhanced public role of the 'dictatorship of the proletariat' concept: can we pair this with the views of a knowledgeable right-wing or centrist representative of the Social-Democracy? Aside from Kautsky (who will appear in the next section), there are three candidates.

(1) Surely Eduard Bernstein must have had something to say on the

subject? His own party, the ISDP, first adopted the twin slogans while he was still a member: didn't he protest, or at least comment? After all, twenty years before, he had denounced the 'dictatorship of the proletariat' as "antiquated"—and it was now the latest rage; he had condemned it as an atavistic "reversion" to "a lower civilization"—and now for the first time it was becoming a power in contemporary politics.

He had a good opportunity to deal with the question when arrangements were made by a sponsoring organization for him to give a lecture on "What Is Socialism?" at the great Philharmonic Hall in Berlin before a large audience. The date was: December 28, 1918.

This was no ordinary Saturday evening. A few days before, there had been a fatal clash between the government's troops and the People's Marine Division in the Marstall barracks, after Ebert and Scheidemann had given General Lequis the green light to fire upon the revolutionary-discontented sailors, eleven of whom had been killed and many wounded. Three days before Bernstein's lecture, a protest rally of 30,000 workers and soldiers had taken place to demonstrate against the "counterrevolutionary" attack on the sailors; the *Vorwärts* building had even been occupied for a while by a furious crowd. The very day of the lecture, the Independents had publicly repudiated all connection with the "slaughter" of the Marine Division and decided to resign from the government, leaving the Social-Democrats in coalition with the counterrevolutionary generals; the same day, a Berlin party assembly of the ISDP had witnessed a widening of the split between its right and left wings.[40] The beginning of the "January days," which ended with the murder of Luxemburg and Liebknecht, was only about a week away . . .

As Berlin and all Germany teetered on the edge of an explosion, Bernstein got up in Philharmonic Hall and—this, I'm afraid, is the entire point—gave a lecture that he might have offered ten years before, or fifteen; severely academic, and almost entirely uninterested in the history that was being made around him. In the fifth and last section, to be sure, dealing with "The Why and How of the Realization of Socialism," he deviated from the timeless tone of the lecture enough to take pride in a recent act of his own: he had boasted to the capitalist class (he told his audience) that everything was currently "peaceful" and "legal" and not a hair had been mussed on anyone's head![41] (How too-too utterly civilized!) His main conclusion was a reiteration: "There can be more socialism in one good factory law than in the statification of several hundred enterprises and plants."[42]

Of course, in this lecture *sub specie aeternitatis* there was not a word about 'dictatorship' or the councils or anything else vulgarly related to the revolution going on.

For the next possibility we have to look a couple of years ahead. In the summer of 1921 he gave a series of lectures at the University of Berlin, published as *Der Sozialismus Einst und Jetzt* (Socialism Yesterday and Today). The 'dictatorship' question did come up in the last chapter, "The Bolshevik Variety of Socialism"; the passage is remarkable only for its lack of content. The 'dictatorship of the proletariat' theme, wrote Bernstein, "has been dogmatically interpreted by the Bolsheviks": a good beginning, but he was not moved to give any undogmatic interpretation of his own, or indeed say anything about it whatsoever.[43]

All this has been a long way of saying that Bernstein made no contribution to our subject, and that it is a fact to marvel at.

(2) The only other right-wing Social-Democratic theoretician who needs mentioning in this connection was Heinrich Cunow, who published an essay on "Marx und die Diktatur des Proletariats" in the *Neue Zeit* in 1920. It had the merit of directly confronting the Left Independent and Spartacist (or Communist) invocation of the 'dictatorship of the proletariat' as Marx's view; it even quoted Loci 11 and 12 (both by Engels). The substance of Cunow's thesis was mainly that Marx favored only rule by a majority, and that he was against minority dictatorship.

> Unfortunately neither Marx nor Engels thoroughly expressed their views on how they thought about the dictatorship of the proletariat; but still from certain statements their opinion can be seen fairly clearly.
>
> To begin with, it must be established that Marx and Engels, in general, did not take up the question whether, when a *minority* of the proletariat captured political power, this minority should use terrorist-dictatorial measures to maintain its rule.

We see that Cunow (like Lenin) was apparently oblivious of Engels' direct discussion of this aspect in his "Program of the Blanquist Refugees of the Commune" (Locus 8). Cunow's article went on:

> For them, in the *Communist Manifesto* it was a question not of a particular section or party of the proletariat, *but of the proletariat as a whole*. They

assumed that the proletarian movement quickly grows bigger and bigger, brings the great mass of the population behind it, *and then only,* when it has become the decisive majority, does it move to take over the state machinery. . . . In Marx's view, the proletariat will win power only *when it embraces the great majority of the population.*[44]

This was elementary for all concerned; but the sticker was: what then did the 'dictatorship' term mean? Even this right-wing Social-Democrat could explain it solely in terms of *suppression:*

> . . . by dictatorship he did not understand arbitrary regimentation by a minority of workers, but the energetic utilization of the power position of the great proletarian majority without mercy against capitalist resistance. In this sense he speaks also of a dictatorship of the bourgeoisie in the present-day constitutional state and of a replacement of this dictatorship of the bourgeoisie by the dictatorship of the working class.
>
> The word 'dictatorship' does not here have the meaning of "forcible rule of a minority," but means the ruthless carrying out of the will of the majority in face of a refractory capitalist minority . . .[45]

There was no other Social-Democratic theoretician in Europe who made a serious attempt to grapple with Marx's thought. In this period, after all, we are entering upon the era—perfected after another world war—when there ceased to be *any* concern with theory in the neo-social-democratic movement.[46]

(3) Let us now drop the qualification "in Europe." There *was* a serious effort made, by a social-democratic theoretician of approximately Kautsky's persuasion, to work out Marx's thought: an effort far superior to Kautsky's, for that matter. It came in America, from a man who is so unjustly undervalued that he is customarily treated with disdain by the ignorant. He was certainly one of the most knowledgeable Marxists in the old American Socialist Party, though essentially a Kautsky-type reformist in ideology. This was Morris Hillquit.★

★Trotsky's sneering dismissal of Hillquit, in *My Life,*[47] has been influential in misleading leftists; but this passage is evidently based on general ignorance of Hillquit's writings. Trotsky's political hostility is well based on Hillquit's political standpoint, which Trotsky *did* know, but it would have been better served by analysis rather than by the invective of contempt. One should know that Hillquit's reaction to the Russian Revolution and the postwar revolutionary upsurge was the opposite of Kautsky's: while Kautsky hurtled to the right, Hillquit was driven to the left—which, for him, meant toward centrism. Until the party split in late 1919 Hillquit worked as legal adviser for the Soviet Government Information Bureau in the United States.

Hillquit's attempt to synthesize a leftist approach to the new post-war era of revolution can be seen best in his 1921 book *From Marx to Lenin*. It took up the hard questions, with an intelligent and informed eye on Marx's views, which he sought to understand and explain. This book was easily the best-informed and most sophisticated social-democratic exposition of the problems we are interested in, of all those published in the postwar period.

The little book had chapters on Marx's view of socialist revolution, "Marx and Engels on Russia," the Russian Revolution, "Violence and Terror," and the International question. But the three central chapters that concern us were Chapters 6 to 8: "The Dictatorship of the Proletariat," "The Function of Communist Dictatorship," and "Soviets or Parliament?" The first of these chapters was the only writing published (as far as I know) clearly explaining that Marx used 'dictatorship of the proletariat' to mean a workers' state, the proletariat in political power.

> Marx and Engels have at different times described the transitional period of working-class political domination as the "Rule," the "Power" or the "Sway" of the workers. They have also characterized it as the *Dictatorship of the Proletariat* and the Bolsheviki have chosen the latter phrase to describe the political character of the present revolutionary regime in Russia.[48]

This understanding of the term is repeated elsewhere in the chapter.

Hillquit's approach is didactic—the book has the tone of an educational handbook or textbook. He expounds the analogy with the 'dictatorship of the capitalist class'; he explains that "The Dictatorship of the Proletariat, contrary to widespread popular assumptions, is not the antithesis of Democracy." He argues (against Kautsky, whom he refutes from time to time) that bourgeois democracy is not a nonclass system of abstract political equality; that working-class democracy also has to be regarded as a "class institution," exercised however by a majority; and he ends the chapter with the presentation of Lenin's thought (from *State and Revolution*) that democracy is also a *state*, organized for class coercion, which will disappear only with the disappearance of class distinctions.[49]

He quotes Lenin's view that dictatorship means an authority "not bound by *any* law," and (being a highly competent lawyer) handily refutes this definition, as well as Kautsky's. True, his discussion of the "etymology" of the term is weak and confused, because he depends on

the Lenin-Kautsky confusion, but he winds up throwing the ety-
mological consideration out of court anyway.[50]

His chapter on the "Communist Dictatorship" gives ample evidence
that the Bolsheviks were defining their 'dictatorship of the proletariat'
as a dictatorship of the ruling party; but, unlike Kautsky, he tries to
show how this attitude was related to specific Russian conditions. In
his attitude toward the Soviet government he reflects the then position
of most American socialists in giving it critical support, while denying
that all of its characteristics were automatically applicable internationally. In fact, his sympathetic stance is very much like that taken
coevally by the German Independents. His chapter ("Soviets or Parliament?") on the council system as an internationally applicable governmental form of the dictatorship of the proletariat poses the essential
issues as clearly as anything written for decades afterwards.

There was a "steel wire" analogue for Hillquit too. During these
years Hillquit stretched his mind *in terms of state theory* as far as a
reformist possibly could, without passing the elastic limit. When the
revolutionary pressures of the time eased up, Hillquit snapped back.
Even before this, in the fights inside the Socialist Party, he fought
against the procommunist Left Wing for control of the organization;
but there were many issues involved in these factional struggles beyond our own narrow focus on only one.

Whatever one's evaluation of Hillquit and his role in the power
struggle, it is undoubtedly true that his attempt to occupy a middle
ground—to straddle, if you will—made it possible for this educated
Marxist to see and explain the theoretical issues in ways that others
refused to recognize. In any case, the power struggle is now long over,
but the book *From Marx to Lenin* remains the single most significant
contribution by the center-left of the Social-Democracy to the analysis
of Marx's and Lenin's views on the 'dictatorship of the proletariat.'

5. The View from Kautsky

In the immediate postwar period Kautsky's flat-out hostility to the
government of the Russian Revolution was shared only by the extreme
right wing of the Social-Democracy, including the leadership of the

SDP. For this political current Kautsky provided a theoretical structure with a series of anti-Bolshevik polemics.*

A large part of Kautsky's writings in this field naturally took up the broad problems of the Russian Revolution and socialist theory, but our narrower focus restricts us to the following questions.

(1) *Marx references.* Kautsky's handling of the Marx-Engels texts contributed to discrediting his approach, for he avoided facing the facts so assiduously that he could be charged with *de facto* falsification. In *Die Diktatur des Proletariats* he quoted only Marx's Locus 9 *(Critique of the Gotha Program),* in such fashion that a reader was led to believe this was the only time Marx ever used the term; he also referred, without quoting, to Engels' Locus 11 (about the Paris Commune).[51] In another chapter of this work, he wrote to the same effect: the Bolsheviks "remembered opportunely the little phrase *[Wörtchen]* 'the dictatorship of the proletariat,'" which Marx used in a letter in 1875."[52] This compounded the offense, for to call Marx's critique of the party program a "letter" made it sound like a personal letter, whereas the document was written as an internal political circular for the party leadership.

Kautsky could not have hoped to get away with this mode of presentation since Lenin's *State and Revolution* (which cited four loci) had been published a few months before he wrote his own brochure. After all, Kautsky was no ordinary reader of Marx: he was supposed to be *the* Authority on Marx's writings. Was he really unaware of the passages in Marx's *Class Struggles in France?* Hadn't he already seen Marx's 1852 letter to Weydemeyer and noticed the striking paragraph? How could he have forgotten Engels' "Program of the Blanquist Refugees of the Commune"—original or reprint?

It was one thing to argue that quotations from Marx did not settle

---

*These began with the following brochures: *Die Diktatur des Proletariats* (Vienna, 1918), written in early August; *Demokratie oder Diktatur* (Berlin, 1918), a revised version of the preceding, dropping some chapters on Russia, written after the November revolution in Germany; *Terrorismus und Communismus* (1919); *Von der Demokratie zur Staatssklaverei* (1921), a polemical reply to Trotsky; *Die proletarische Revolution* (1922). Subsequent books also dealt with Russia in whole or part. Kautsky's fullest discussions of Marx's relation to the 'dictatorship of the proletariat' came in the first-named, Chapters 5 and 10, and in a compilation *Social Democracy versus Communism* (New York, 1946), edited and translated from writings by Kautsky published in German in 1932–1937, including a Section 2 titled "Marxism and the Dictatorship of the Proletariat." (For English editions, see the Bibliography.)

the matter; it was another thing to conceal them; and anyway, quotations from Marx *did* settle one thing, viz., Marx's views. In his later *Social Democracy versus Communism* Kautsky added only Engels' Locus 12 (on the Erfurt Program) to the two others,[53] even though by that time much more had been published on the subject. Even in his 1927 opus on *Die materialistische Geschichtsauffassung* he persisted in referring to "the phrase [*Wort,* not *Wörtchen* this time] of the dictatorship of the proletariat which Marx once gave utterance to, though only on occasion, without saying what kind of state constitution he had in mind for this political condition"[54]—just as if he had learned nothing but, unlike the Bourbons, forgotten much. Incidentally, Bernstein's 1922 book *Der Sozialismus Einst and Jetzt,* mentioned in Section 4 above, echoed Kautsky by locating the 'dictatorship of the proletariat' in "a place in Marx's letter on the Gotha Program" as if this were the sole *Wörtchen* by Marx.[55]

(2) *Meaning of 'dictatorship.'* In Chapter 5 of his 1918 brochure, Kautsky raised the question of what Marx conceived 'dictatorship of the proletariat' to mean. Strangely enough, he adopted the new definition invented by Lenin!

> Taken literally, the word [dictatorship] signifies the suspension of democracy. But taken literally it also means the sovereignty of a single person, who is bound by no laws.[56]

This allows him to conclude that Marx could not have "thought of dictatorship in the literal sense." (No more than others did Kautsky have any idea that the word had changed in meaning between 1850 and 1918.) Thus he combined some of the worst aspects of Lenin's misinterpretation together with his own.

In his later book, he retreated to vagueness:

> Marx and Engels never explained why they characterized this condition as a "dictatorship," although it was to spring from democracy. I assume they used the expression to denote a strong government.[57]

Vagueness would have been preferable to what he proceeded to write next: "Karl Marx was not the only one to speak of the dictatorship of the proletariat. This idea is much older than Marxism." He thereupon trotted out Babeuf, the "Jacobin reign of terror," and Blanquism as early exponents of the dictatorship of the proletariat, neglecting to cite where they advocated it as distinct from dictatorship *tout court.*[58] In the course, he cryptically informed the reader that Babeuf's was to be "a proletarian dictatorship, but not the dictatorship *of* the proletariat . . ."[59]

We should add hurriedly that by the time he published *Die proletarische Revolution* in 1922, he had made an about-face on a little point, apparently related to his definitions. Whereas in *Die Diktatur des Proletariats* he had claimed to be *for* the 'dictatorship of the proletariat' in Marx's meaning,[60] by 1922 he had amended this to say he was against it: "The dictatorship of the proletariat as a means for the introduction of socialism must therefore be rejected." For he had now discovered that "the dictatorship of a class, conceived as a state institution," meant that *any and every worker* could freely "plunder and mishandle" any bourgeois at will.[61] This passage is the best evidence I know for the opinion held by some that Kautsky's old age was dimmed by senility.

(3) *Governmental form or state type.* Kautsky had a strong argument at his disposal, and it is instructive to see how he mishandled it. As we have seen, Lenin and the Bolsheviks were more and more interpreting 'dictatorship of the proletariat' to mean certain special governmental forms, institutions, or policies—coercion and violence, disfranchisement possibly, weighted votes, etc., or some combination of these. Marx, on the other hand, had used 'dictatorship of the proletariat' only to mean a workers' state; the phrase pointed only to the *class* content of the revolutionary transitional state after the conquest of power, and said nothing about the forms that might be found to outfit a workers' state. Even where Marx did have views on what such forms might be, it was not the term 'dictatorship of the proletariat' that communicated these views.

Kautsky understood that such a distinction existed, but when he tried to write it down, only half of it emerged. He wrote that in the *Critique of the Gotha Program* Marx "had indeed only intended to describe a political *condition,* and not a *form* of government."[62] Not a form of government—yes; but—a "political *condition*"? This was the vague locution that he substituted for the obvious term: *workers' state.*

Wonderful is the logic of politics! Why was Kautsky unable to write down the obvious fact that Marx's little *Wörtchen* meant a working-class state? The answer is: because, in 1918, this was precisely what the leftists (Spartacists and Left Independents) were demanding of the Social-Democratic leadership, and what both the Majority Social-

Democrats and Right Independents were repudiating—with the support of Kautsky.

If Kautsky had really counterposed *Marx's* views to those of the Bolsheviks in interpreting the *Wörtchen,* he would have found himself supporting the politics of—Rosa Luxemburg. This he was not about to do. Instead of counterposing the idea of a workers' state as against the "dictatorial" interpretation of the *Wörtchen,* he went in an entirely different direction: he counterposed *abstract democracy* (which will be considered in the next point).

This is also clear from another passage in which he substituted "condition" for the obvious "workers' state." In the *Critique,* he wrote, Marx speaks

> not of a form of government, but of a condition which must everywhere arise when the proletariat has conquered political power. That he was not thinking of a form of government is shown by his opinion that in England and America the transition might be carried out peacefully. Of course, democracy does not guarantee a peaceful transition. But this is certainly not possible without democracy.[63]

Let us leave aside that Marx and Engels knew an initially "peaceful" achievement of power might be followed by civil war to defend the power against a "proslavery rebellion,"[64] that is, counterrevolutionary violence. In citing a "peaceful" acquisition of power as if it constituted a "form of government," Kautsky's argument took a couple of leaps, which alone made sense of what looked like a non sequitur. He was assuming that a "peaceful" acquisition meant maintenance of the existing *parliamentary* forms of government, which in turn was his formula for abstract democracy. In the above passage, all of these ideas were mixed up in one mingle-mangle of concepts, with the idea of a workers state blurred behind the vagueness of a "condition."

Very soon, however, all of this became irrelevant to Kautsky, for in his *Proletarische Revolution* of 1922 he repudiated the very concept of 'class dictatorship.' We have already exhibited this in part under point 2 above; but even more direct evidence was his roundhouse statement that

> the description of the bourgeois state as the "dictatorship of the bourgeoisie" is one of the most absurd fictions that our age has produced.[65]

Although this was directed against the "crudeness of Bolshevist thought," was it possible that he had forgotten how Marx and Engels *and the entire socialist movement* had long used this concept far more frequently than the 'dictatorship of the proletariat'? Note that he did not merely express disagreement with it: it was now "absurd," that is, incomprehensible.

(4) *Democracy and abstract democracy.* We have seen[66] that, already by 1918 but sporadically, Lenin began to break out with attacks on "democracy" which treated that sorely tried term as a purely and inherently *bourgeois* category, wholly negative in content. This tendency was even more virulent among other Bolshevik propagandists. The formulation began cropping up that 'democracy' was at best a meaningless noise, that there was only bourgeois democracy or proletarian democracy, the latter being synonymous with 'proletarian dictatorship.' Kautsky's formulations about 'democracy' were not refuted but only hooted down.

On this, as on other matters of general theory, we have only a limited point to make here, only what is necessary for our subject. If the claim that 'democracy' unqualified meant nothing was valid, then much of Lenin's prewar writing was nonsense. But it can be shown, rather, that the claim was nonsense: for it was often accompanied by another claim, namely, that proletarian democracy was a thousand times *more democratic* than bourgeois democracy.[67] If this is so, there has to be some common content that is being compared, some generalized notion of 'democracy' against which both forms of class democracy are measured. Whatever this is, it is your definition of general democracy.*

The existence of general criteria for democracy does not in the least impugn another conclusion: that in social reality any given social institution is decisively conditioned by its class character. Institutions reflect bourgeois democracy or proletarian democracy—true. General democratic criteria—yes; abstract-democratic institutions—no. *This* was the positive content of the Bolshevik formulations. In contrast, Kautsky's chapters on the 'dictatorship of the proletariat' were chockfull of assumptions about *abstract democracy.* One can approve Kautsky's approach or refute it; but (a) one cannot approve it on the basis of Marx's theory of the state; and (b) one cannot refute it on the basis of

---

*To illustrate: My own general definition, put briefly, is this: that is more democratic or less depending on how it facilitates *control from below* in all social institutions. But the main point does not depend on this or any other definition.

the newly burgeoning Bolshevik theory of the meaninglessness of 'democracy.'

(5) *General applicability of the 'dictatorship.'* We have pointed out that Lenin came up against an inconvenient fact about Marx's view. Marx clearly asserted that any and every workers' state was necessarily a 'dictatorship of the proletariat'; yet at times Lenin attempted formulations which implied that the term was *not* generally applicable.[68] Kautsky's exposition collided with this difficulty too.

After the above-quoted passage about the misty "political condition" called the 'dictatorship of the proletariat,' Kautsky wrote that "Marx had somewhere said that under certain circumstances things might come to a dictatorship of the proletariat . . ."* *Under certain circumstances:* this means that, under some other circumstances, there would not be a 'dictatorship of the proletariat.' Yet Kautsky had quoted the one locus that was most explicit on precisely this point: it "can be nothing but *the revolutionary dictatorship of the proletariat*"[69]— "nothing but," Marx had written. In any case Marx could have meant nothing else: for he emphasized the necessity of establishing a workers' state a thousand times more often than he ever mentioned the 'dictatorship of the proletariat.' *Every* workers' state was a 'dictatorship of the proletariat,' or else it meant nothing.

(6) *The council system and the 'dictatorship.'* Toward the end of his *Diktatur des Proletariats* Kautsky got onto a point on which he might have been effective; once again he mishandled it. But we have to get it right, for it was a question on which the Bolshevik propaganda of the time was as confused and confusing as Kautsky's argumentation.

The question was this: was the council system (soviet system in the general sense, *Rätesystem*), as a *form of government,* a necessary and inevitable and "permanent" feature of the dictatorship of the proletariat? Was it a special Russian peculiarity? Was it inevitably international, but not "permanent"? In short, what was the exact relationship in theory and practice between the two elements of the "twin slogans" so often heard together?

I have no intention of taking up answers to this question; it is so important that it needs a book to itself. My sole reason for raising it

---

*In this same paragraph Kautsky has other statements which might or might not mean that Marx viewed the 'dictatorship of the proletariat' as "unavoidable for the transition to socialism." It doesn't much matter.

is—to set it aside. *For this question was not covered by Marx's view of the 'dictatorship of the proletariat,'* which embraced *no* idea about specific governmental forms as a necessary part of the concept. We must repeat a point already made: whatever views Marx had on governmental forms were not thought of by him as expressed by the term 'dictatorship of the proletariat.'

But wasn't there an exception? For in Locus 12 Engels stated that the democratic republic was "the specific form for the dictatorship of the proletariat."[70] The following remarks are necessary:

(a) The context indicated that this opinion of Engels was directed specifically to Germany, though he would probably have applied it to the advanced capitalist countries at least. But it was a *separable* conclusion that he had come to about the 'dictatorship of the proletariat': a conclusion precisely about the *forms* suitable for a particular conjuncture of time and place. Without changing one's interpretation of 'dictatorship of the proletariat' as meaning a workers state in general, some other Marxist could conceivably come to the opinion that some other form might be suitable on some other continent.

(b) As we have pointed out before, 'democratic republic' is not a very specific form: it leaves open the question of widely varying types of governmental institutions or forms. If Luxemburg's comrades had established a German workers' state on the basis of the Workers' and Soldiers' Councils, it would have been not only a workers' republic but a democratic republic. There is no incompatibility in meaning between 'soviet republic' (*Räterepublik*) and 'democratic republic.' The later claims of incompatibility were derived from the degeneration of the Bolshevik theory of democracy into the theory of the "meaninglessness" of the term 'democracy' used by itself.

(c) A Marxist could conceivably conclude, as Kautsky in fact did, that a workers' state could be founded on the basis of *parliamentary* institutions: if not as a general proposition (Kautsky's course), then at least in singular circumstances (as in England after a "peaceful" revolution in a world situation already dominated by socialism). A Marxist's opinion on this score should, to be sure, be based on Marx's theory of the state as applied to and qualified by the experiences of social revolution in our time; but whatever one concludes, *the answer is not contained in advance in the term and concept 'dictatorship of the proletariat.'*

Now Kautsky found it impossible to take the attitude sketched here, for a simple reason: he himself held a conclusion on this question that was as thoroughly dogmatic and doctrinaire as any put forward by one of the muscle-bound-Marxist types that flocked to the Third International in 1918–20. This was the conclusion that Kautsky had come to even before the war: that the Social-Democrats' road to power *had* to be through parliamentary forms and channels and no other.[71]

This sort of petrified dogmatism is usually ascribed to ultraleft types only, quite erroneously; and so it must be understood that—to go back to the questions with which we started—Kautsky merged, or blurred, the questions together as much as anyone.

(7) *The Beleaguered Fortress.*—Another respect in which Kautsky's standpoint was congruent with retrograde tendencies among the Bolsheviks was his refusal, or inability, to think of the 'dictatorship of the proletariat' in Soviet Russia as one beleaguered fortress in the midst of a wider war, the European revolution.

Insofar as the Russian Bolsheviks held on to the Beleaguered Fortress view of their position, it was easier for them to think of their deviations from workers' democracy as exceptional, emergency distortions of the "steel wire," which could hopefully be expected to snap back whenever the international pressure was removed. On the other hand, insofar as they thought of the Russian Revolution in isolated national terms, they were encouraged to rationalize their dictatorial innovations as a new standard of revolution. The end result of the latter mode of thought was the Stalin theory of 'socialism in one country,' which operationally meant the rationalization of bureaucratic dictatorship in that one country.

In page after page, and work after work, Kautsky posed the problems of socialist revolution in Russia in its national isolation—as starkly as any Stalinist did later. And he came to the same conclusion—only with value signs reversed (minus instead of plus). He insistently argued that Marx thought of the 'dictatorship of the proletariat' as a rule by the majority (true) whereas the working class was a smallish minority in Russia (true), but he found it as uncongenial as Stalin to think of the revolution in Russia as a victory in one beleaguered fortress, which could be saved by the revolution in Germany (which he opposed). For Kautsky no less than everyone else, the last problem of the 'dictatorship of the proletariat' was its internationalization and internationalism.

The Beleaguered Fortress model of the 'dictatorship of the proletariat' could be held valid only as long as the steel wire remained elastic.

6. Lenin's Rejoinder: A New Stage

Kautsky's attack on the Russian Revolution and the Soviet government, an attack cast in the form of a theoretical disquisition on the 'dictatorship of the proletariat,' evoked a series of replies from the Bolshevik side. Like Kautsky's assaults, all of the defense documents were less concerned with Marxist theory than with current vindications. As before, we cannot follow all the issues in this debate; we focus, again, on what was happening to the concept of 'dictatorship' and of the 'dictatorship of the proletariat,' though this was a by-product.

The defense was led by Lenin's reply to Kautsky's *Diktatur des Proletariats*, a reply published in October 1918 with the title *The Proletarian Revolution and the Renegade Kautsky*. One must remember the circumstances under which this *Anti-Kautsky* was written, as the revolution hung on to life in a war against fourteen invading armies of the imperialist intervention, all of whose political leaders claimed to be defending democracy against dictatorship. As one of his colleagues reminisced later, Lenin "was literally burning with anger," "sitting up every day till late at night," writing the polemic.[72]

The result was a booklet which flamed with indignation, and whose vituperative tone no doubt delighted those who were already convinced; but in terms of theoretical argumentation it was perhaps the worst work Lenin ever published.* Its content has to be picked out of an enveloping fog of invective. Many of the points involved have already been discussed. The aspect that concerns us is the way in which this work represented a stage in the developing line of post-1917 Leninism on 'democracy'—the line whose beginnings we noted in Chapter 4.[74]

---

*This had happened before when Lenin allowed anger and indignation to swamp his reasoning processes. The best preceding example was his 1915 article against Trotsky on 'revolutionary defeatism,' a case I have discussed elsewhere in similar terms.[73]

In hindsight, the important step taken by Lenin's *Anti-Kautsky* was its implicit repudiation of the idea that the proletarian or socialist revolution was a revolution of the majority of the people, as the *Communist Manifesto* had emphasized.[75] It was only implicit because Lenin did not actually assert the repudiation here. What he did was to cite *Kautsky's* espousal of majority revolution, and, by merging it with Kautsky's accompanying line of 'abstract democracy,' denounce it as bourgeois liberalism alien to Marxism. There were several passages of this sort,[76] which would require considerable space to quote and analyze; but we can make do with one which came along in a summary vein.

> If we argue in a liberal way, we must say: the majority decides, the minority submits. . . . Nothing need be said about the class character of the state in general . . . a majority is a majority and a minority is a minority . . . And this is exactly how Kautsky argues.[77]

Here the 'majority' question is blurred together with the 'abstract democratic' method of denying the class character of states, so that *both* can be tossed out with one rhetorical gesture.

In the nearest approach by Lenin to confronting the obvious challenge, he reported that Kautsky asked, "Why do we need a dictatorship when we have a majority?" Lenin replied that "Marx and Engels explain" that a dictatorship is needed in order to suppress the bourgeois resistance to the revolution.[78] (Let us leave aside the fact that neither Marx nor Engels ever linked this consideration to 'dictatorship.') Study the reply and you see Lenin's method of short-circuiting the argument. What was needed to suppress the bourgeois resistance was the *workers' state;* but neither Marx nor Engels *nor Lenin before this* had ever counterposed this revolutionary need to the concept of majority revolution.

What Lenin wanted to tie to Marx's tail was a concept of 'class democracy' which he set forth, early in his *Anti-Kautsky,* in paradigmatic terms as follows:

> . . . the ancient state was essentially a *dictatorship of the slaveowners.* Did this dictatorship abolish democracy *among,* and *for,* the slaveowners? Everybody knows that it did not.[79]

This was the model of a *class dictatorship* which was at the same time a *class democracy,* a democracy for the ruling class only; but this model concerned a case where the ruling class was a minority of the people ruling in the interests of a minority. By adopting this as his model for the 'dictatorship of the proletariat,' Lenin "forgot" that Marx and all Marxists had always insisted that this was precisely the respect in which a *workers'* state was basically different from all previous ruling-class states.

Adopting the slaveowners' state as the paradigm for the 'dictatorship of the proletariat,' Lenin reconciled himself to the unprecedented notion that a 'dictatorship of the proletariat' could just as well be the state power of a minority suppressing a majority as vice-versa. We need hardly expound the motivation driving him to this break with Marx: the minority position of the Russian proletariat isolated from the European revolution.

This theoretical enormity was blurred in the process of argumentation by a device that cropped up all through the *Anti-Kautsky:* confusion of the 'transition period' in general with the short period of *civil war,* pitched battle for the conquest of power or its consolidation. It was and is easy to argue that the niceties of democratic procedures could not be observed between armed camps engaged in killing each other; or at any rate this was a separate question, inquiring into the special emergency exigencies of a workers' power in the midst of heavy civil war. But it is only when this situation is over that the constructive period of the workers' state (dictatorship of the proletariat) begins. As we have pointed out,[80] the genesis of post-1917 Leninism was in good part the transformation of notions about emergency deviations into theories about "inevitable" revolutionary norms. We have a special case of this process, as Lenin transformed the desperate necessities of civil war into the basic characteristics of the whole transition period from the initial conquest of power to the final building of socialist society.

Here is an illustrative passage:

> In these circumstances, in an epoch of desperately acute war, when history presents the question of whether age-old and thousand-year-old privileges are to be or not to be—at such a time to talk about majority and minority, about pure democracy, about dictatorship being unnecessary . . . ! What infinite stupidity . . . ![81]

On the one hand, this talked of an "epoch," on the other hand of "desperately acute war," thus *telescoping* the idea of civil war into that of the whole epoch of the transition from capitalism to socialism. There were many such passages.

Then, much farther along, came an antidote clause, completely separate from the above argumentation. If the Bolshevik government, Lenin wrote, had in 1917 "decreed" the "introduction of socialism" into the rural districts, "without a temporary bloc with the peasants in general,"

> that would have been a *Blanquist* distortion of Marxism, an attempt by the *minority* to impose its will upon the majority . . .[82]

The concept of majority revolution had been denounced a few pages back as a purely bourgeois-liberal notion; now Lenin remembered something he used to say about Blanquism: this was the product of a guilty (theoretical) conscience.

Before leaving Lenin, we should note his intention, a year later, to write an extensive work on "The Dictatorship of the Proletariat," this title being affixed to a bare outline which was never written up.[83] The phrases jotted down in this outline are only suggestive of how Lenin was trying to think the issues out. Under Part II, Point 12, headed "Decision by Majority," he noted:

> Its conditions: real equality (culture), real freedom.[84]

What was this precondition, "culture," which was necessary before one could have "decision by majority"? Since the outline says nothing more, let us juxtapose a passage about "cultural level" from Lenin's report to the party congress in March 1919:

> We can fight bureaucracy to the bitter end, to a complete victory, only when the whole population participates in the work of government. . . . Apart from the law, there is still the level of culture . . . The result of this low cultural level is that the Soviets, which by virtue of their program are organs of government *by the working people,* are in fact organs of government *for the working people* by the advanced section of the proletariat, but not by the working people as a whole.
>
> Here we are confronted by a problem which cannot be solved except by prolonged education.[85]

This passage, of course, reminds us of Lenin's later remarks about the "deformed workers' state." But a "deformed workers' state" means a deformed or distorted 'dictatorship of the proletariat'—a 'dictatorship of the proletariat' which has been stretched like a steel wire. If "decision by majority" was conditioned on the development of a more "cultured" and educated proletariat, who meanwhile wielded the dictatorship?

If one follows the outline further down, the effective answer comes along under Part III, Point 25, with the brief notation:

Dictatorship of the *revolutionary* elements of the class.[86]

Lenin never filled out this outline, which obviously pointed toward the conscious acceptance of a minority dictatorship by the party; but others did.

By this time, Lenin had canonized the watchword of 'dictatorship of the proletariat' as the holy of holies of Marxist theory: "the very essence of proletarian revolution," "the key problem of the entire proletarian class struggle."[87] Exactly what this meant was as blurry and shifting as his definition of dictatorship; but in the sequel, this claim became beatified as one of the new "principles" of Marxism that Marx had never heard of. It became customary in the Comintern to expatiate on something called Marx's "*theory* of the dictatorship of the proletariat"—presumably different from merely Marx's views on the role of a workers' state—though the attribution of such a "theory" to Marx was as much an invention as the "theory of increasing misery," the tenet that "the end justifies the means," the principle of "the worse the better," and other well-known ectoplasmic constructs of Marx-mythology.

7. End of the Line

The international debate reached a sort of zenith, quantitatively speaking, in 1920, after Kautsky's 1919 *Terrorismus und Kommunismus* precipitated a series of rejoinders by Bolshevik Party spokesmen. A full account of this debate would require two things I lack: ability to read Russian and space to detail the arguments. But for our present purposes we do not need a full account. Let us survey four important and representative documents available in English:

- L. Kamenev, *The Dictatorship of the Proletariat*. A thin, sixteen-page pamphlet, dated June 1920.
- Karl Radek, *Proletarian Dictatorship and Terrorism*. A sixty-page booklet.
- N. Bukharin, "The Theory of the Dictatorship of the Proletariat," first published in 1919 in a collection of articles by various hands.

• L. Trotsky, *Terrorism and Communism*. Published in 1920 as a book-length polemic against Kautsky's work of the same title.★

A common characteristic was that these writers asserted things that Lenin was still skirting around. I think none of them understood the extent to which they were jettisoning Marx's Marxism—and they certainly cared less about this consideration than did Lenin. This attitude was affected by two factors: they were more brashly swayed by the heady feeling that the whole universe of socialist thought was now brand-new and "up for grabs," a virgin snowfield waiting for new footprints; and they could feel this way all the more uninhibitedly because, compared with Lenin, they were much more ignorant of Marx's views. For example . . .

Trotsky habitually eschewed Lenin's pattern of anxiously inquiring into "what Marx said" on any given question; and of course this attitude can be explained as a justified aversion to quotation-mongering. The fact is, however, that typically Trotsky not only didn't care "what Marx said," but often didn't know what Marx thought—an ignorance which can also be vindicated, perhaps, provided he did not attempt to expound what he was ignorant of. In *Terrorism and Communism* Trotsky came a cropper at the first attempt. Referring to Locus 12 he wrote that Engels "obstinately defended the dictatorship of the proletariat as the only possible form of its control of the state."[88] This formulation would have been impossible for Engels, for whom the 'dictatorship of the proletariat' was not a *form* of the workers' state but a synonym for the workers' state.

Similarly: Kamenev plainly had no idea that the Russian party was the *only* one that had programmatically adopted the 'dictatorship of the proletariat.' "The dictatorship of the proletariat," he wrote, "appears in the programmes of the Socialist parties not later than the seventies of the nineteenth century."[89] This real ignorance of the history of Marxism and the movement should be borne in mind when we come, below, to exegeses on the Paris Commune.

More crudely than Lenin, these leaders and theoreticians plainly

---

★See the Bibliography for publication data on these titles. In addition, it is worth consulting the 1919 Soviet textbook, *The ABC of Communism* by Bukharin and Pre-obrazhensky, which had long sections on the 'dictatorship of the proletariat.' A later stage was represented by the 1923 textbook, *Elements of Political Education* by Berdnikov and Svetlov.

equated the 'dictatorship of the proletariat' with the period of civil war. Kamenev flatly called the 'dictatorship' a "period of warfare," "an epoch of undisguised warfare, and armed clash . . ."[90] Bukharin wrote down that "in an era of civil war, the model of state power is bound to be dictatorial." His further discussion was predicated on "the protracted nature of a lengthy civil war . . ."[91]

The new style of repudiation of 'democracy' was pushed forward in ever cruder language. *Because* Kautsky kept vaunting the Paris Commune as 'democratic,' Radek and Trotsky fell into the trap: they "refuted" Kautsky by turning on the Commune with arguments (specious) purporting to show that it was *anti*democratic—as antidemocratic as Soviet Russia, you see. The Commune, asserted Radek, was "an insurrection against the results of universal suffrage in France," "an insurrection . . . for the purpose of winning special rights for Paris . . ."[92] Trotsky's book had an atrociously twisted chapter on the Commune that stood Marx's *Civil War in France* on its head.[93]

It was Trotsky who went farthest in throwing 'democracy' out with the bathwater, that is, with Kautsky's 'abstract democracy.' It was also he who went farthest in advocating the deformation of workers' democracy in state affairs: this in the course of the Trade Union question (statification of trade unions) and the militarization of labor. (See Deutscher's biography, last chapter of Volume 1.) This indeed was the real context for his theoretical enormities in *Terrorism and Communism*, but it is not my subject. It is necessary to emphasize that it was not only a question of some momentary slip in Trotsky's thinking, but, rather, his adoption for a whole period of a deep-going and systematic break with Marx on the nature of a workers' state. One pays for theoretical sins. When Trotsky later accepted the label 'workers' state' for Stalin's totalitarian regime, solely and exclusively because it maintained statified property, he was continuing his lamentable record of separating the concept 'workers' state' ('dictatorship of the proletariat') from the question of working-class control from below ('rule').

As in the case of the Commune, it was partly the *Agin'* syndrome: whatever Kautsky was for, one had to be against; whatever Kautsky praised had to be bourgeois liberalism or worse. In his anti-Kautsky, *Terrorism and Communism*, Trotsky simply equated majority revolution with the "fetishism of the parliamentary majority."[94] (Was there a fetishism of the Soviet majority?) His analysis bottomed out with a new version of the old theory of the impossibility of majority control due to the *corruption* of the masses by present-day society. The masses of the people are held, through the educational system, "on the verge of complete ignorance," with "no opportunity of rising above the level" of "spiritual slavery"; the capitalists "corrupt, deceive, and terrorize the more privileged or the more backward of the proletariat itself." The function of the dictatorship of the proletariat was to reverse this situation . . . And somehow Trotsky did not realize that this argument destroyed any concept of a class dictatorship wielded even by a minority proletariat.[95]

Kamenev invited opponents to find a model in the capitalist war-time dictatorships, which carried out the gigantic task of organizing worldwide war. "Was this achieved," he demanded to know, "by means of democracy? By the means of parliamentarism? By means of the realisation of the sovereignty of the 'people'?" No, it was not; the world at war was "governed by the methods of dictatorship," "by openly passing over to the methods of dictatorship."[96]

The 'dictatorship of the *party*' was ever more candidly advocated as the reality behind the 'dictatorship of the proletariat' concept.

> . . . in reality—and if we do not play with words—such an organisation [such as a general staff in battle] can only be the political party of the proletariat; i.e., an organisation of the most advanced, revolutionary elements of the proletariat, united by their common political programme and an iron discipline.[97]

Thus Kamenev. Here, as on some other questions, Trotsky was the worst. Only the party must have "the final word in all fundamental questions." He carried the process another step forward, or down-ward:

> Further, our practice has led to the result that, in all moot questions, generally—conflicts between departments and personal conflicts within departments—the last word belongs to the Central Committee of the party. This affords extreme economy of time and energy; and in the most difficult and complicated circumstances gives a guarantee for the neces-sary unity of action.[98]

As he had argued in 1904 (with signs reversed), it would be still more economical of time and energy to impose not merely the dictatorship

of the Central Committee but indeed the domination of the Secre-
tariat.

> The revolutionary supremacy of the proletariat presupposes within the
> proletariat itself the political supremacy of a party, with a clear pro-
> gramme of action and a faultless internal discipline.[99]

One day he would find out where the "fault" lay in this dream of
efficiency. Meanwhile he thought that

> it can be said with complete justice that the dictatorship of the Soviets
> became possible only by means of the dictatorship of the party.

Otherwise the Soviets would be "shapeless parliaments of labor."
With this phrase (though probably not thought through as such)
theory descends a level: it is no longer "parliamentary" democracy
that is impugned but any *representative* democracy. The power of the
party, Trotsky went on to admit, is "substituted" for the "power of the
working class"—but this 'substitutionism' is a bit too frank and he
takes part of the confession back.[100]

If our subject were broader, it would be necessary to continue
detailing this theoretical debacle of Trotsky's, but it is perhaps enough
to say that he goes on to argue for the outright "militarization of
labor."[101]

Enough, for our purposes: we are so far from Marx's original
concept of class dictatorship that there is no connection. But one last
concept must be reported on: the main contribution of Bukharin's
essay to the burial of democracy.

Why (Bukharin asked) were Communists formerly in favor of
democracy, indeed bourgeois democracy, but are now opposed to it?
Simple: it's the difference in the "epoch." In the past we had to present
our "class demands" in "a 'democratic' form," but now we are free to
speak our true mind. In the past the "proletariat"

> was forced to demand, not freedom of assembly for *workers,* but freedom
> of assembly in general . . . , freedom of the press in general . . . etc. But
> there is no need to make a virtue of necessity. Now that the time has
> come for a direct assault on the capitalist fortress and the suppression of
> the exploiters, only a miserable petty-bourgeois can be content with
> arguments about "the protection of the minority."[102]

In the past, you see, we had to mask our real view so that our
opponents would not know that we were lying when we pretended to

support democratic rights on principle; we had to conceal that we demanded minority democratic rights only for ourselves and would deny them to others once we got the whip hand. . . . What a gigantic conspiracy it must have been, for the entire Marxist movement to have carried out this fraud! Bukharin claimed that the movement had lied in the past, and he was telling the truth now: but in fact, of course, no such absurd conspiracy had ever existed—Bukharin was lying *now,* to cover up a 180° turn in his view of democracy. In any case, with this line of argumentation, no one could believe him and his likes then or now. A movement that printed this drivel was discredited for the future as for the past.

In these ways, well in the van of Lenin, Bukharin and Trotsky took the *theoretical* lead in gutting socialism of its organic enrootment in the mass of people. When Stalin took another lead, the lead in organizing the socioeconomic counterrevolution in class power, the "juridical" basis in theory (to use Trotsky's later expression) had already been laid. That fact is not gainsaid by another, namely, that when Bukharin and Trotsky looked upon their handiwork, they started in horror and scrambled away from it in another direction.

But now we are very near the point where the locution 'dictatorship of the proletariat' simply became a code word for a species of totalitarian dictatorship, and hence devoid of any independent theoretical interest. The end of our story coincides with the end of an era in the history of socialism.

Special
Notes

Charles Bonnier on 'Dictatorship of the Proletariat'

A Note to Chapter 2, Section 6, Page 53

One of the better-known statements at the end of the nineteenth century, purporting to explain the 'dictatorship of the proletariat' to French socialists, came from Charles Bonnier. After appearing in the Guesdist party organ *Le Socialiste* in 1897, it was in good part reprinted both in Compère-Morel's *Grand Dictionnaire Socialiste* in 1909 and in Vérecque's *Dictionnaire du Socialisme* in 1911.[1]

Bonnier was a French socialist writer, later a university lecturer. He joined the French Workers Party (Guesdists or "Marxists") when he was about 17; besides being active as a party militant, he became a contributor to the socialist press. His best-known book, *La Question de la Femme,* was also published in 1897. For many years he was a lecturer at Oxford University, while remaining in close touch with his friend Jules Guesde; and so Engels had to deal with him as a sort of representative of the French party. By the same token, Bonnier must have had many opportunities to talk with Engels. He also followed German socialist literature.

Engels had been dead for two years when Bonnier wrote a three-installment article for *Le Socialiste* on "La Conquête des Pouvoirs Publics."[2] The "Bernsteiniad" had barely started at this time: Bernstein's first *Neue Zeit* articles on "Problems of Socialism" started appearing in 1896, continuing through the next two years; his book came out in 1899. When Bonnier published his first installment in December 1896, there was still no general realization of what had happened to Bernstein. Bonnier's article did not mention Bernstein, but I surmise that he may have been provoked to take up the subject of "political power."

Bonnier's second installment started with emphasis on the necessity of "the triumph of the proletariat: the more or less violent death of the society based on the capitalist system." It was in the third installment, published on January 10, 1897, that he undertook to explain the 'dictatorship of the proletariat.' The following excerpts constituted most of this installment.

> If there is one necessity that clearly emerges from studying the facts and that imposed itself rigorously on the founders of scientific socialism, it is that of the Dictatorship of the Proletariat. Many socialist militants, including the best intentioned, reject the term even if they accept the thing itself, claiming that this term dictatorship has taken on, in our history, a sense of monopolization and violence. Thus we have to make clear here what was meant by Dictatorship of the Proletariat both by Marx and Engels, who devised the term, and the French Workers Party, which has inscribed it on its banner.*
>
> Dictatorship means government, more or less prolonged, by one part of society, by a class, over the other classes, at the precise time when ordinary laws are no longer in force. Thus it was that in Rome, at times of great danger, a man was invested with all the powers of the Republic, both civil and military, for a definite period. Likewise, on certain occasions the Doge in Venice or the principal magistrate in the Italian republics. In modern times we have had the Jacobin Dictatorship, and then, as its fatal outcome, the Eighteenth Brumaire of Bonaparte.
>
> These were the excessive and, so to speak, crude forms of Dictatorship which have stuck in the minds and imagination of the crowd. But if we separate the thing itself from its surroundings, from its appearance, we see, behind a greater or lesser degree of violence, military apparatus or civil proscription, always the same indispensable element: illegality. Indeed, let anyone show us in modern history a single government that at its origin did not have this character of illegality, of dictatorship.

Citing Taine's *France Contemporaine,* Bonnier goes through a number of cases that illustrate the foregoing thesis. (I would remark, very much aside, that any new government that did *not* begin by changing the rules of legality would be, by the same token, not very new; hence Bonnier's thesis is self-proving.) The article then concludes as follows:

---

*The Guesdist party "inscribed it on its banner" only metaphorically; the phrase was *not* in the party program.

What is called a regular government is a myth, in the bourgeois period, and it does not deceive even the president of the Chamber. Now all these governments have been—to put it moderately—governments of dictatorship during the first third of their duration. They governed against the mass of the population, and it was only when by friction between governors and governed and by habituation there was established a sort of compromise that the machine could function in a somewhat satisfactory fashion, until the next upset came.

Well then, when we speak of revolutionary Dictatorship, we mean simply that there will come a time when the proletariat conscious of its strength will seize power by force (in one form or another), and, so long as it has not accomplished its mission and justified its reason for existence, it will be in a "condition of Dictatorship." It is not by free choice that it will get to that point but by historical necessity.

What will distinguish it from other governments will not be its seizure of power but the manner in which it will exercise it. Whereas the other governments had the mission only of representing and affirming a class, the proletariat will destroy classes and absorb them into the collectivity. But to do this, in its seizure of the Dictatorship and as long as it exercises it, it is necessary for it to be distinct and personal, separated both from its friends who have only a confused notion of the necessity of its historical role and consequently could stand in its way, and from its enemies who will do their best to prevent it from being fulfilled.

Bonnier's statement, near the end, that the "dictatorship" will be "personal" is very surprising. Indeed, I think it must have been a typographical or other error, for the formulation "impersonal dictatorship of the proletariat," used especially by Vaillant, was heard in France when the term was used.

Special Note B

Supplement to Chapter 5

The following notes concern the period covered in Chapter 5; but while they are of some interest, they might be digressive if inserted in that chapter.

1. Trotsky and Party Dictatorship

Trotsky never specifically reviewed the opinions he expressed in *Terrorism and Communism.* His views on the famous Trade Union Question (statification of trade unions and militarization of labor) were intimately associated with his theoretical views on the 'dictatorship of the proletariat'; they are discussed in a long list of easily available works. For a picture of the government's position, one can do worse than read the last chapter in Isaac Deutscher's first volume of his Trotsky biography.[1]

But nowhere does Deutscher even mention Trotsky's publication of *Terrorism and Communism,* though it was a substantial book and quite well known. Deutscher bases his analysis of Trotsky's "Jacobin" view of dictatorship on the internal party developments. For example, he quotes Trotsky's explicit endorsement of the party's right to "assert its dictatorship even if that dictatorship temporarily clashed with the passing moods of the workers' democracy"; to place "the workers' right to elect representatives above the party" would be making "a fetish of democratic principles."[2]

In his 1937 pamphlet *Stalinism and Bolshevism,* Trotsky appeared to make an attempt to vindicate the post-1917 Bolshevik position, in general, on the 'dictatorship of the proletariat.' Denying that "the political 'sins' of Bolshevism" are "the source of Stalinism," he conceded that

> it is absolutely indisputable that the domination of a single party served as the juridical point of departure for the Stalinist totalitarian system.[3]

But he argued that the *prohibition* of other parties was viewed as an exceptional measure, "a measure of defense of the dictatorship in a backward and devastated country, surrounded by enemies on all sides." This it certainly was to begin with, but even in 1937 Trotsky refused to confront the theoretical (not juridical) structure that he and others had erected by 1920.

He referred to left-wing critics who charged that "the Bolshevik . . . replaced the dictatorship of the proletariat with the dictatorship of the party; Stalin replaced the dictatorship of the party with the dictatorship of the bureaucracy."[4] His reply asserted that the comparison was "empty," but this reply avoided mentioning the words "dictatorship of the party." All he argued was the need for the *leadership* of a vanguard revolutionary party—a proposition which in any case required that its exact content be specified. His concluding argument was:

> The fact that this party subordinates the Soviets politically to its leaders has, in itself, abolished the Soviet system no more than the domination of the conservative majority has abolished the British parliamentary system.[5]

Something is "empty" indeed: when one party dominates the British Parliament at some juncture in the party battles for a majority, the institutions of bourgeois democracy are not abolished or eviscerated but, instead, provide the arena for another party to dominate tomorrow (with all of the qualifications pertaining to *bourgeois* democracy). But this was precisely the "fetish" of democratic rights, the "liberalistic" and "abstract" (or "formal") democracy that Trotsky and others sought to stamp out as incompatible with the 'dictatorship of the proletariat.'

The question is not whether these "sins" of the Bolsheviks constituted the *source* of Stalinism, because the source of the Stalinist counterrevolution in Russia was socioeconomic, and has to be explained in terms of class relations, especially the rise of the state bureaucracy as a ruling class (the socioeconomic development which Trotsky denied).

Just as the enormous pressures of the post-1917 period helped to produce the socioeconomic conditions out of which Stalinism was born, so too did these pressures (forces) give rise to the initial *theoretical rationalizations* on the basis of which Marxist theory was twisted out of shape. In this way, something still called "Marxism" was reworked to provide the Stalinist counterrevolution with suitable theoretical instruments.

Before Stalinism could use a bastardized "Marxism" as its formal political-theoretical basis, that "Marxism" had to be ground up and hashed and reprocessed and warped into something different. The first stage of this process was the historical function of such works as those considered in the last section of Chapter 5. In all this, the role of the 'dictatorship of the proletariat' concept was simply that of a victim.

2. The Russian Anarchists in the Post-1917 Period

> It is not generally appreciated that the idea of dictatorship played any role in anarchist thinking, but many anarchists were embracing the notion of the dictatorship of the proletariat.[6]

So writes D'Agostino of the post-1917 period in Russia, in his informative work *Marxism and the Russian Anarchists*. Of course, we have seen (in *KMTR* 3) that 'dictatorship' played a heavy role in anarchist thinking, and so this development is not a surprise. It characterized a section of the Russian anarchist movement which wanted to occupy a position in Soviet life as a recognized tendency.

Victor Serge's memoirs mentioned a prominent case. Iu. S. Roshchin (aka Grossman),

> who in the old days of 1906 had been the theoretician of "motiveless terror" . . . , became a syndicalist and a friend of Lenin and Lunacharsky; he was developing a libertarian theory of the dictatorship of the proletariat.[7]

Avrich reports that there was a tendency of "Anarcho-Bolsheviks" including not only Roshchin-Grossman but also Bill Shatov, A. G. Zhelezniakov, A. Iu. Ge, and D. I. Novomirsky.

> . . . in Moscow alone, two sizable groups of fellow-traveling Anarchist-Communists were organized with the object of forging links of amity and cooperation with the "proletarian dictatorship."[8]

These elements included Apollon Karelin and the Gordin brothers. In 1918 Karelin, leading a group of pro-Soviet anarchists called the All-Russian Federation of Anarchist-Communists, won a seat on the Soviet Central Executive committee. He argued that the Soviet dictatorship was a necessity to defeat the reaction and a transitional stage toward an anarchist society. A. L. and V. L. Gordin founded another group of Anarchist-Communists in 1920: the "universalists," which endorsed the "dictatorship of the proletariat" more or less on the same grounds as Karelin.[9]

D'Agostino relates that many Russian anarchists greeted Lenin's *State and Revolution* as providing a common ground for anarchism and Marxism (presumably on the basis of its stress on "smashing the state machinery").

> Many anarchists made the last step and accepted the dictatorship of the proletariat as the political form of the transition period. The anarcho-syndicalist Spanish CNT temporarily adhered to the Third International and called for the dictatorship of the proletariat.[10]

G. P. Maximov (who later edited a Bakunin collection[11]) was a leader of the Russian anarcho-syndicalists in the revolutionary period, and at this time (until his exile in 1921) developed a theory on the relationship of syndicalism to Bolshevik communism. It included the idea of a transition period which would be the 'dictatorship of labor.'[12] Another group of syndicalists, represented by Alexander Schapiro of the *Golos Truda* group, also spoke of an anarchist interpretation of the 'dictatorship of the proletariat.'[13] But Maximov was critical of the Makhno anarchist movement on the ground that it was a "personal dictatorship"; and other anarchists, such as Volin and Arshinov, attacked the "authoritarian methods" of the Makhno movement.[14] Later, in the 1920s and early 1930, Peter Arshinov developed a view that D'Agostino calls "a kind of left-Stalinist *Makhnovshchina*": a theory reconciling anarchism and Marxism, including the 'dictatorship of the proletariat.' In 1930 he quit his paper and returned to Russia, vanishing in the Stalin purges.[15]

3. A Brace of British Braintrusters

Our last chapter, on "The International Debate," deals only with rational and relatively informed representatives of the various viewpoints in the post-1917 period. In a sense, this gives a false impression. For example, the British left-winger who wanted to find out what the argument was all about was not likely to read either Kautsky or Lenin; he might read, say, Eden and Cedar Paul . . .

The Pauls were best known as prolific translators,★ but in the postwar period they joined the British Communist Party and came forward as theoreticians, especially in a book titled *Creative Revolution* (1920).[16]

Here they expounded Marx and Lenin on the 'dictatorship of the proletariat' in exactly the same way as the most ignorant part of the Tory press—but with approval. The Soviet regime was an "oligarchic" dictatorship, in which a minority of intellectuals fortunately suppressed the ignorant majority of proletarians and peasants. Their chapter titled "The Dictatorship of the Proletariat" explained that "the absolute rule . . . will have to be a dictatorship *over* a large section of any proletariat." The socialists, who can *never* constitute a majority before the revolution, "will seize the reins of power and will hold sway while the remolding of social institutions is engendering a quasi-universal socialist mentality."[17] (Simon-pure Babouvism.) The "iron law of oligarchy" and H. G. Wells' attacks on democracy prove that democracy is impossible or imaginary; it is really "mob rule" plus "plutocracy."[18] The "proletariat" means "those who are proletarian by status merely" or "those who are proletarian by revolutionary convic-

---

★I must add that their translations of Marxist works are unreliable and quite bad, in every case I have had occasion to check. They have a theory of translation, popular in England, which demands that the translator reprocess the author's thought like a city editor rewriting a cub reporter's stuff. Marx, reprocessed through the Pauls' brain cells, gains something in the translation, but what it gains is not Marx.

tion."[19] The book is peppered with suggestions that Marx and Engels were second-raters and Lenin a rather tiresome Russian compared with—well, modern Communists.[20] Materialism is rejected for Bergsonism. And this exponent of oligarchic despotism by a minority is also sympathetic to anarchism and syndicalism.[21]

This hurried appreciation of the Pauline opus does not begin to plumb the depths of political illiteracy and ignorance that yawn in every chapter of the book. Yet it must be kept in mind that in every country the new Third International was being swamped with recruits who had equally ignorant (if different) notions about the 'dictatorship of the proletariat' and the allied doctrines of something called 'Marxism.'

It is time for comic relief. This is hard to find in our subject, but there was the discovery of the 'dictatorship of the proletariat' by Sidney and Beatrice Webb, the founders of Fabianism. As is well known, in the 1930s they, together with the third of the Fabian triad, Bernard Shaw, became convinced Stalinists, firmly persuaded that in Russia Stalin, having buried the Russian Revolution as a mistake, was building the Fabian social order in all its purity. This point of view they put forward at length in their work *Soviet Communism,* which demonstrated by industrious search through the Propaganda Ministry's handouts that the beneficent nature of the Stalinist state was proved by Stalin's own documents. But at first they found the phrase 'dictatorship of the proletariat' a stumbling block. "We frankly confess," they wrote in their book, "that we do not understand what was or is meant by this phrase."[22] This is one of the most sensible statements they made, and it is too bad they did not stick with it. But in 1941 they issued a new edition of their two-volume work, with a new introduction which was also published separately under the title *The Truth About Soviet Russia.* By this time, evidently, their education had advanced.

It was in the *The Truth* that the Webbs mused that

> how far Premier Stalin and his colleagues . . . approve of the continued existence of the Third International is unknown.[23]

And that wasn't the only thing unknown to them. It transpired that the Webbs, after writing nearly 1,200 pages of solid type on Soviet Communism, did not know the name of the ruling party or the most elementary facts of its history:

The All-Union Party (of Bolsheviks), which today is its official title, first appeared in 1898 at Minsk, as the result of a cleavage in the Social Democratic Party of Russia, two separate parties emerging . . .[24]*

However, they now undertook to explain the 'dictatorship of the proletariat':

> Karl Marx had suggested a "dictatorship of the proletariat," to be followed, in some undefined way, by a "classless society." When fanatical followers argued among themselves what exactly these phrases meant, and appealed to their leader, Karl Marx is reported to have observed, "I am not a Marxist" . . .[26]

This may remind us of the Monty Python sketch about a character named Karl Marx. On the other hand, a few pages further, the Webbs launched an explanation about 'democracy' and 'dictatorship,' modeled on the once-famous sketches in which Sid Caesar imitated a German professor:

> . . . political democracy represents all the inhabitants of a given territory. It is necessary to emphasize this plain and indisputable fact, because the supremacy of the political democracy over industrial democracy not only angers the anarchists . . . but upsets those who believe in "workers' control" or the "dictatorship of the proletariat." What is still more surprising is that some avowed believers in political democracy suspect the duly elected deputies of becoming, somehow or other, "dictators" of a peculiarly sinister type.[27]

Anyone who enjoys this should look up the ruminations on the Russian dictatorship by Bernard Shaw, set down after he visited Russia in 1931. His unfinished manuscript, published as *The Rationalization of Russia,* was filled with gleeful approval of the Stalin government's wise custom of shooting anyone "dangerous to the dictatorship of the proletariat."[28] Even the Webbs' divagations on democracy look profound alongside Shaw's septuagenarian drivel about the need to smash all "liberties" and the paramount duty of states to kill opponents— "Bang, bang!" he repeats mindlessly.[29] Perhaps he learned about "Marxism" by reading the Pauls' *Creative Revolution.*

---

*Since the reader has probably not written 1,200 pages on the subject, we should explain that the 1898 Minsk congress was the first, unsuccessful congress of the Russian Social Democratic Labor Party; the cleavage between Bolshevik and Menshevik factions of the RSDLP took place in 1903 in London; and the name Communist Party did not "appear" in Russia until 1918. The Webbs added the opinion that the Bolshevik party was first "led by Plekhanov and afterwards dominated by Lenin."[25]

4. *France: Charles Rappoport*

The preceding section needs an antidote; it is not only a question of clowns. There were serious Marxist thinkers who illustrated the deep theoretical disorientation engendered in the postwar period.

When the Russian Revolution took place, one of the most highly-thought-of students of Marxism in the ranks of the French movement was Charles Rappoport. Russian-born, originally a Narodnik, Rappoport was an émigré student in Bern until 1887, active in Berlin until 1895; then, having moved to Paris, he became a French citizen in 1899, at the age of 34. He was active in the Fédération des Socialistes Révolutionnaires till 1905, thereafter in the united Socialist Party, as a left-wing Marxist writer of note. In World War I he supported the antiwar wing, hailed the Bolshevik revolution, joined the Communist Party in 1920, and sat on its Executive Committee till 1922. He quit the CP in 1938 and rejoined the Socialist Party, remaining until his death in 1941. His books, like *La Philosophie de l'Histoire comme Science de l'Evolution* (1903), are no longer well known, but they gave him a reputation as a knowledgeable Marxist.

In 1920, the first year of the French CP's existence, Rappoport explained "Marx et la Dictature du Prolétariat" to the readers of the party's theoretical journal. It was the best that France could do.

Rappoport made no attempt to treat Marx's references to the subject, nor even to mention them. The bulk of the article expounded the historical-materialist basis of political power. When he came to the term 'dictatorship' (which, he remarked, was a word Marx used "rarely") he was comfortable only in explaining the meaning of capitalist dictatorship.

> . . . political power means the State armed to the teeth. But *the armed political power at the disposal of a minority* (even in the presumed interest of a majority) *is dictatorship.* Thus, the domination of the possessing classes has, by definition, a dictatorial character.[30]

This definition of 'dictatorship' left no room for a dictatorship by a majority class. It appears that Rappoport could not make any sense out of the latter idea and, instead, spent most of the remaining space exposing the deceptions of bourgeois democracy (which was much the easiest thing to do).

But what about the 'dictatorship of the proletariat'? The proletarian dictatorship is different from the bourgeois dictatorship because (1) it is temporary and does not claim to be eternal, and (2) it tells the truth about itself, without hypocrisy or lies, whereas "the dictatorship of minorities for the benefit of minorities needs the ignorance and lack of consciousness of the masses to maintain itself."[31]

"Dictatorship of minorities for the benefit of minorities": this calculated phrase was Rappoport's way of introducing his real point:

> Marx nowhere says that in order to take Power, that is, exercise their dictatorship, the communists have to wait until the time when they become the majority.

Obviously he wants to say that the 'dictatorship of the proletariat' means a dictatorship by a (proletarian) minority *for the benefit of the majority*—but still, a minority dictatorship. But he refrains from putting this part of the truth on the line. Instead, he explains away the well-known passage in the *Communist Manifesto:*

> In the Manifesto, he [Marx] contents himself with the fact that the Communist party represents, obviously, the vital interests of the immense majority . . .[32]

So in the end our truth-seeker finds himself distorting the Manifesto's plain statement that the proletarian movement *is* the "independent movement of the immense majority . . ."[33]

Yet he has just written a hymn of praise to Truth, because the dictatorship of the proletariat

> tells it the way it is. It has nothing to dissimulate, for its task is to abolish all class domination. It needs the whole truth as it needs air [etc.] . . .

And so it strangled in lies.

5. The Left-Socialist Revival of the 1930s

A word may be of interest on a phenomenon which is outside our time frame. Around 1933–1934, in direct reaction to the collapse of the European Social-Democracy in the face of fascism, the 'dictatorship of the proletariat' watchword was revived in the Second International (called the Labor and Socialist International). The resuscitated slogan clearly played the role of a shibboleth: it symbolized a turn to the left away from the bankrupt parties that were discredited after capitulating without a fight.

In Germany, an underground socialist group—originally founded in 1931 as a secret organization of dissident Communists and left Social-Democrats—became active in 1933 under the leadership of Walter Löwenheim, who under the pen name "Miles" published a pamphlet titled *Neu Beginnen*. (English and French translations came out in 1934: in America *Socialism's New Beginning*.) The Miles group, or "New Beginners," stated with great vigor that the revolutionary goal should be a socialist state in which "the socialist party must concentrate the whole power of the state exclusively in its own hands," and which would have a "centralized form as a party state."[34] Although the form 'dictatorship of the proletariat' was not used in the pamphlet, it was at the center of controversy in the various wings of the now illegal Social-Democratic movement, no part of which withstood the flight from the discredited Social-Democratic tradition.

> This crisis of democratic socialism within the German labor movement and the renaissance of Marxist social revolutionary traditions had repercussions throughout the international Socialist movement. In the Labor and Socialist International, and among the parties affiliated with it, the old problem of whether evolution or revolution, democracy or dictatorship of the proletariat were the right way to socialism, was debated with renewed fervor as a consequence of the developments in Germany.[35]

So wrote the historian Edinger. The greatest impact came in the first period, and was reflected in a manifesto adopted in January 1934 by the old-line Social-Democratic Executive in exile—*even* by them. It described a dictatorial transition period completely in terms of what was thought to be the revolutionary Marxist spirit.[36] To be sure, the old-liners welched on this document as soon as they felt a little strength behind them, but the would-be left-wing New Beginners made this approach their hallmark.[37]

What was meant by this so-called return to Marxism was explicitly antidemocratic, an "educational dictatorship." "Democracy" had failed; the masses had proved too immature and irrational to support a democratic regime; "once a revolutionary minority got power, it could and should use its position to assure itself a popular majority *before* restoring democratic processes"; the new movement should be a "revolutionary elite organization" uniting Social-Democrats and communists.[38] Kautsky, who was simply standing pat, complained that not Lenin but Hitler "has caused many a Social-Democrat to despair of democratic methods and to conclude that the only road to a socialist order is through a dictatorship, as in Russia."[39]

A similar development swamped the Austrian socialists, led (and channeled into ambiguity) by Otto Bauer. Soon after the victory of the Austro-fascists and the destruction of the legal Social-Democratic movement, Bauer declared for a "dictatorship" in the transition period; the Social-Democrats could now fight only for a dictatorship of the proletariat.[40] In the course of 1934 he repeated that the revolutionary objective could only be the dictatorship of the proletariat "as a form of transition to socialist democracy," and the newly named "Revolutionary Socialists of Austria" adopted this language with approximately the same understanding as the German left wing.[41]

As mentioned, this language reverberated through the Socialist International. At its Paris congress that year, the representatives of the Jewish Bund of Poland introduced a resolution which included approval of the "dictatorship of the revolutionary party," at least in some versions—but after the delegates of the American Socialist Party voted for it, they were told that it was a mistranslation and should have read "dictatorship of the proletariat."[42]

It was not accidental that the American delegates saw nothing wrong with the formula 'dictatorship of the revolutionary party.' A strong faction had developed in the American Socialist Party, called the "Militants," which wanted to be "left wing," indeed revolutionary Marxist. (It was a classic centrist development, but that is another story.) This centrist group, which was going to win the party from the "Old Guard" the following year, was freely putting its own version of "revolutionary dictatorship" down on paper. "Dictatorship of the party" occurred in the official program of the faction, the so-called "Boundbrook program" (named after a conference held in Boundbrook, New Jersey). It was also written down in a socialist cultural magazine which they issued briefly around this time, titled *Arise!* Socialist Party "Militants" back from visiting Spain reported that the socialist left around Largo Caballero was for a "dictatorship of the party" as the famous transition stage.[43]

In the case of this American development, if not in the European cases, I can explain why the 'dictatorship of the party' formula appeared. The reason was long ago given by Dr. Johnson in answer to the woman who asked him to account for an error in his dictionary: "Ignorance, madam, pure ignorance." These fresh-baked proponents of a "dictatorship of the party" were violently anti-Leninist and anti-Bolshevik. On the other hand, the Marxist left wing then in the Socialist Party, which dominated the youth organization and regarded the militants as centrists, pointed out that the idea of a "dictatorship of the party" was antidemocratic. A paradox!

Reference Notes

Titles are given in abbreviated form; full titles and publication data are provided in the Bibliography. Book and article titles are not distinguished in form. Where only the author's name is given, there is only a single entry in the Bibliography. Page numbers apply to the edition cited in the Bibliography. Volume and page are usually separated by a colon: for example, 3:148 means Volume 3, page 148.

For Chapter 1, as explained in the Preface, all references are to my *Karl Marx's Theory of Revolution*, Volume 3, "The 'Dictatorship of the Proletariat.'" Only the page numbers are given, e.g., 148 instead of *KMTR* 3:148.

All initials are identified in the Index.

1. *The 'Dictatorship of the Proletariat' in Marx and Engels.*

 1. The Roman *dictatura:* 14–16.
 2. Martial law, etc.: 16–19.
 3. In the 20th century: 20–21. Survey of pre-1789 usages: 23–26.
 4. The French Revolution: 27–32; Marat: 33–38; Robespierre: 39–40.
 5. Babouvist movement: 44–51. Marx and Babouvism: 183–89.
 6. Blanquists; the myth of the Blanquist origin of the term: 51–60.
 7. Early Utopians, esp. Cabet: 60–64. Dézamy, Morrison, etc.: 65–68. Cabet in 1850: 177–81.
 8. Louis Blanc: 69–73.
 9. Weitling: 60–61, 83–85.
10. Bakunin in 1848: 86–89.
11. Cavaignac's dictatorship: 74–82.
12. Marx in the 1848 revolution: 92–105.
13. This paragraph: 107.
14. Guizot: 108–09.
15. Donoso Cortés: 109–11.
16. Stein: 112–16.

17. 'Despotism' in Marx: 117–21.
18. This paragraph: 121–25.
19. Military dictatorship: 125–29.
20. A number of such figures, including the "dictators" of the Democracy: 129–41.
21. Bakunin: 142–49; some Bakuninists: 154–56.
22. Lassalle: 150–54; Schweitzer: 156–60.
23. Comte, Hyndman, Jones: 161–65.
24. This paragraph: 169–71.
25. *Communist Manifesto:* 171–73.
26. Chartists: 173–74.
27. Concept of class rule: 174–77.
28. Periodization: 168–69.
29. Locus 1, first chapter: 271–73. (For the use, in this work, of 'dictatorship' alone: 266–71.)
30. Locus 1, second chapter: 273–74.
31. Not summarized here is *KMTR*'s extensive discussion of Blanqui and Blanquism with relation to Marx; in *KMTR* 3, see Chaps. 9–10, 17–18, and Special Note B.
32. Blanqui as bogey: 276–79.
33. Locus 1, third chapter: 274–76.
34. SUCR's collapse: 294–304.
35. The full text: 281–82; discussion: 282–86.
36. Willich and SUCR: 319–22.
37. On the Blanquist group involved here: 286–94.
38. Basic thesis: 323–25.
39. Lüning and *NDZ:* 329–33.
40. Lüning's views and critique: 334–41.
41. Marx's letter to *NDZ:* 341–44.
42. Weydemeyer: 370–73.
43. Weydemeyer's article: 373–77.
44. Marx's letter: 377–79.
45. The occurrence of 'dictatorship of the proletariat' in Marx's *Herr Vogt* is discussed in 380–84.
46. Marx's analysis of the Commune: 412–19.
47. The split in the Commune over 'dictatorship': 422–26.
48. Blanquists and the International: 427–31. The case of Vermersch: 442–26.
49. Blanquist split: 432–35.
50. Banquet speech: 447–51.
51. Locus 6: 451–54.
52. The Blanquist pamphlets: 432–38.
53. Locus 7: 454–57.
54. Locus 8: 462–64.
55. Locus 9: 464–69.
56. Republication of Marx's "Critique": 475–76.
57. Locus 10: 474–75.

58. Commotion in the party: 476–82.
59. Locus 11: 483–86.
60. The interpretation: 488–89.
61. Locus 12: 486–88
62. 'Democratic republic': 489–93.
63. Engels' proposal: 494.
64. Voden's memoirs: 495–97.

2. Second International Sketches (Still Life).

1. On Lafargue, see *KMTR* 3, Chap. 20, Sec. 1.
2. E. Bernstein, *Evolutionary Socialism,* 146.
3. On Liebknecht in 1891, see *KMTR* 3, Chap. 20, Sec. 4.
4. W. Liebknecht, "No Compromise, No Election Deals," in the pamphlet *On the Political Position of Social-Democracy,* 78f.
5. Ibid., 79.
6. Lenin, "Pref. to Russian Trans. of Liebknecht's Pamphlet," *Coll. Wks.* 11:401–07.
7. Wolfe, *Three Who Made a Revolution,* 238.
8. Article "Péguy, Charles," in *Encyc. of the Social Sciences,* 12:55.f.
9. Jaurès, *Etudes Socialistes,* page xxv.
10. Ibid., xxvii.
11. Ibid., xxxiii–xxxiv.
12. Karl Liebknecht, "Die neue Methode," *Neue Zeit,* 20. Jg., 2. Bd., Nr. 23, 1901–02, p. 714f.
13. Longuet's preface to the pamphlet (imprinted Paris, G. Jacques, 1900) was published in *Le Mouvement Socialiste,* Jan. 15, 1901; my citation is from p. 76.
14. See *KMTR* 3, Chap. 2, ref. note 21.
15. Sombart, *Socialism and the Social Movement,* 69.
16. Vérecque, 142f.
17. In this section, quotations from Mehring and Kautsky are from Paul Frölich's introduction to Vol. 3 *(Gegen den Reformismus)* of Luxemburg's *Gesammelte Werke,* 1925, not to be confused with the later *Gesammelte Werke;* page 24. See also Lidtke, 328; Laurat, *Marxism and Democracy,* 56 fn.
18. Marx, *Civil War in France,* in *MESW* 2:220; see also references to parliamentarism on 218, 219.
19. Ibid., 217.
20. Marx & Engels, Preface to the 1872 edition of *Communist Manifesto,* in *MESW* 1:99.
21. See the conclusion of Engels' 1886 preface to the English edition of *Capital,* Vol. 1, in *MEW* 23:40.
22. For the complex title of this work, see the Bibliography for Kautsky's *Die Vorläufer des neueren Sozialismus.*

23. Kautsky, *Die Vorläufer &c.*, 138. For another translation, see Kautsky, *Communism in Central Europe*, 28.
24. Kautsky, *Bernstein und das sozialdemokratischen Programm*, 172.
25. Ibid.
26. Ibid., 180.
27. Ibid., 181.
28. Kautsky, *Der Weg zur Macht*, 18.
29. Kautsky, *The Road to Power* (Simons tr.), 12.
30. Kautsky, *Der Weg zur Macht*, 20.
31. Luxemburg, *Sozialreform oder Revolution?*, in her *Gesammelte Werke*, 1.1:433.
32. Luxemburg, *Dem Andenken des "Proletariat,"* in her *Gesammelte Werke*, 1.2:317. This is a German translation of the Polish original; the English has been checked against a different German translation in Luxemburg, *Politische Schriften*, 3:34, titled "Der Partei 'Proletariat' zum Gedächtnis," where the last sentence begins, "A precondition of the socialist transformation . . ."
33. Luxemburg, "Die russische Revolution," in her *Gesammelte Werke*, 2:8.
34. Ibid., 9.
35. Luxemburg, *Was wollen wir?* in her *Gesammelte Werke*, 2:47. (Polish title: *Czego chcemy?*)
36. Ibid., 48.
37. Ibid., 89.
38. Luxemburg, *Massenstreik, Partei und Gewerkschaften*, in her *Gesammelte Werke*, 2:153.
39. Luxemburg, "Die Theorie und die Praxis," *Neue Zeit*, 29. Jg., 1909/10, 2. Bd., in her *Gesammelte Werke*, 2:383.
40. Ibid., 410.
41. Luxemburg, "Brennende Zeitfragen," in her *Gesammelte Werke*, 4:279.
42. Ibid., 279f.

3. Plekhanov and Other Russians.

1. Hook, *Marx and the Marxists*, 34.
2. See Chap. 1, Sec. 8.
3. Plekhanov, "Socialism and the Political Struggle," in his *Sel. Phil. Wks.* 1:109f.
4. Lavrov, *To the Russian Social-Revolutionary Youth* (London, 1874), 40–43; quoted by Plekhanov, *Our Differences*, in his Sel. Phil. Wks. 1:302. Italicization follows Plekhanov's text; an interpolation by Plekhanov has been omitted.
5. Hardy, *P. Tkachev*, 201, 257, 272–74; Venturi, *Roots of Revolution*, 426f.
6. Engels, "On Social Relations in Russia," in *MESW* 2:387 [*MEW* 18:556].
7. Plekhanov, *Our Differences*, in his *Sel. Phil. Wks.* 1:303.

8. For the 1892 article, his *Sel. Phil. Wks.* 1:454; for the article "Bourgeois of Days Gone By," in *Le Socialiste,* Apr. 23, 1893, ibid., 1:485.

9. Plekhanov, "Initial Phases of the Theory of Class Struggle," in his *Sel. Phil. Wks.* 2:466.

10. Ibid., 2:472f; see also an article of 1901, ibid., 2:370. There was a mention of the term in 1905, ibid., 3:87.

11. Quoted in Landauer, *European Socialism,* 1:424; for another translation, see Wolfe, *Three Who Made a Rev.,* 235.

12. Wolfe, *Three Who Made a Rev.,* 225.

13. Lenin, "Notes on Plekhanov's Second Draft Program," *Coll. Wks.* 6:51; see also 6:59. About the first draft, cf. *Coll. Wks.* 41:40.

14. Wolfe, *Three Who Made a Rev.,* 235f.

15. Dan, *Orig. of Bolsh.,* 326.

16. Wolfe, 236; Dan, 325; Keep, 122; Lenin, *One Step Forward,* in his *Coll. Wks.* 7:227.

17 This is cited from Lenin, *Coll. Wks.* 42:47, where it is quoted in an article by Lenin published Jan. 4, 1918; however, the italicization (presumably added by Lenin) has been eliminated. Less extensive quotes from Mandelberg's speech may be found in Keep, *Rise of the S.-D.,* 123, and Dan, *Orig. of Bolsh.,* 325.

18. Keep, *Rise of the S.-D.,* 123.

19. Quoted in Wolfe, *Three Who Made a Rev.,* 236.

20. On the myth that Marx believed that "the end justifies the means" *tout court,* see *KMTR* 1:52–54 and 48 fn.

21. Same as note 17 above, ibid., 42:47f. Besides Keep and Dan, Plekhanov's speech is also excerpted in Wolfe, *Three Who Made a Rev.,* 236, and Baron, *Plekhanov,* 242.

22. Schapiro, *C.P.S.U.,* 45f, 47–52.

23. Martov, *Gesch. der Russ. Soz.-dem.,* 79.

24. Dan, 325f.

25. Wolfe, 237.

26. Lenin, *One Step Forward,* in his *Coll. Wks.* 7:227f.

27. Dan, 326.

28. Baron, *Plekhanov,* 243.

29. Ibid., 105.

30. Besides general biographical material on Plekhanov and his personal relations, one should compare Lenin's autobiographical account, "How the 'Spark' Was Nearly Extinguished" (1900), in *Coll. Wks.* 4:333.

31. Martov, "Marx and the Dict. of the Prol.," 64.

32. Dan, *Les Socialistes Russes et la D. de la P.,* 8.

33. Ibid., 9f.

34. Martov, *The State and the Soc. Rev.,* 42 fn.

35. Getzler, *Martov,* 83.

36. Dan, *Orig. of Bolsh.,* 325 f.

37. Dan, *Les Socialistes Russes et la D. de la P.,* 14.

38. Keep, *Rise of the S.-D.,* 24, quoting a work by Axelrod published in 1898.

39. Trotsky, *Stalin*, 78.
40. Keep, *Rise of the S.-D.*, 123.
41. Deutscher, *Prophet Armed*, 90.
42. Ibid., 93.
43. Trotsky, *Our Revolution*, 136f. Here the 1906 pamphlet is called "Prospects of a Labor Dictatorship"; elsewhere it is titled *Results and Perspectives*.
44. Radkey, *Agrarian Foes of Bolsh.*, 41.
45. Ibid., 42.
46. Ibid., 39.

4. Lenin and 'Dictatorship.'

[NOTE: In this chapter, titles are by Lenin unless otherwise ascribed.]

1. Lenin, *Two Tactics of the Social-Democracy*, in his *Coll. Wks.* 9:29.
2. Lenin, "Karl Marx," ibid., 21:71.
3. "Draft and Explanation . . . ," ibid., 2:93+; see esp. 95f, 108.
4. "Draft Program of Our Party," ibid., 4:227+; see esp. 253.
5. "Review; Karl Kautsky . . . ," ibid., 4:193+.
6. *What Is to Be Done?*, ibid., 5:353, 363, 390–91 fn.
7. "Outline . . . ," ibid., 41:40.
8. "Draft Program . . . ," ibid., 6:29. Cf. also "Material for Working Out . . . ," ibid., 41:46.
9. "Notes on Plekhanov's Second Draft Program," ibid., 6:51.
10. Marx & Engels, *Communist Manifesto*, in *MESW* 1:117 [*MEW* 4:472].
11. Ibid., 118 [473].
12. Lenin, "Notes on Plekhanov's Second Draft Program," in his *Coll. Wks.* 6:53 fn. The suspension points at the end are in the text and do not represent an omission.
13. *One Step Forward, Two Steps Back*, ibid., 7:227f, 382f; see above, Chap. 3, Sec. 2.
14. See *KMTR* 2, Chap. 7 (Sec. 2, 3, 6); Chap. 8 (Sec. 4); and page 254; also *KMTR* 3, Chap. 4 (Sec. 2).
15. Lenin, "Draft Resolutions . . . ," in his *Coll. Wks.* 8:195 (editorially dated Feb.).
16. First article: "New Tasks and New Forces," ibid., 8:212; second article: "Ozvobozhdeniye-ists and New-Iskrists," 8:221.
17. "Report . . . ," ibid., 8:385.
18. See the articles in his *Coll. Wks.* esp. at 8:279f, 284f, 293+, 382+.
19. "Report . . . ," ibid., 8:385.
20. For Marx in 1848, see Chap. 1, Sec. 2, or, in more detail, *KMTR* 3, Chap. 4.
21. Lenin, *Two Tactics of the Social-Democracy*, in his Coll. Wks. 9:131.

22. Ibid., 9:84.
23. *Contrib. to Hist. of Ques. of Dict.*, ibid., 31:340 + ; the excerpt is on 346–61.
24. *Victory of the Cadets . . . ,* ibid., 10:245.
25. Ibid., 216.
26. Ibid., 244.
27. Ibid., 246.
28. Ibid., 218, 230.
29. Ibid., 246f.
30. Ibid., 247.
31. "The Proletariat and Its Ally . . . ," ibid., 11:374; "Some Sources of the Present Ideological Discord," 16:90. For examples of "routine" usages, see 16:377, 17:221.
32. "On the Slogan for a U.S. of Europe," ibid., 21:342.
33. "Reply to P. Kievsky," ibid., 23:25.
34. "Caricature of Marxism . . . ," ibid., 23:74.
35. Ibid., 69.
36. "The 'Disarmament' Slogan," ibid., 23:95. For other references in 1916, see 22:153, 356, and 23:165.
37. Ltr, Lenin to Armand, Feb. 3, 1917, ibid., 35:282.
38. "The Dual Power," ibid., 24:38.
39. Ibid., 39.
40. Report, 7th All-Russia Conference of the Party, May 7, 1917, ibid., 24:239.
41. "Epidemic of Credulity," ibid., 25:65.
42. Draft Theses, 7th All-Russia Conference of the Party, May 7, 1917, ibid., 24:256.
43. *State and Revolution,* ibid., 25:404.
44. Ibid., 461f.
45. Ibid., 413, 490.
46. Ibid., 402.
47. Ibid., 487f.
48. Ibid., 463.
49. Ibid., 441.
50. "Can the Bolsheviks Retain State Power?" ibid., 26:94 124f; "Revision of the Party Program," ibid., 26:155, 170.
51. "Theses on the Constituent Assembly," ibid., 26:379, 383.
52. "Plekhanov on Terror," ibid., 42:47f.
53. "Draft Resolution for the C.C. . . . ," ibid., 42:48f10.
54. "Speech, at the Congress . . . ," Jan. 18, 1919, ibid., 28:410.
55. "Fear of the Collapse of the Old . . . ," ibid., 26:401.
56. "Concluding Speech . . . ," ibid., 26:473f.
57. Radkey, *Sickle Under the Hammer,* 144; see also 141.
58. Lenin, "Report . . . ," Jan. 26, 1918, in his *Coll. Wks.* 26:489–91.
59. "Report . . . ," at the Congress, Jan. 20, 1919, ibid., 28:415.
60. See, for ex., ibid., 27:233, 265, 379, and 28:415.

61. "Immediate Tasks . . . ," ibid., 27:263.
62. Report . . . , All-Russia C. E. C. Session, Apr. 29, 1918, ibid., 27:300.
63. "Six Theses . . . ," ibid., 27:316.
64. "Left-Wing Childishness and the Petty-Bourgeois Mentality," ibid., 27:340.
65. "Report on Foreign Policy," ibid., 27:379.
66. Speech . . . , ibid., 28:132.
67. Speech . . . , ibid., 28:170.

5. *The International Debate on 'Dictatorship.'*

1. Sturzo, *Italy and Fascismo,* 54.
2. Nenni, *Ten Years of Tyranny in Italy,* 52.
3. Sturzo, 86.
4. Nenni, 104.
5. Ibid., 106.
6. Quoted in Somerhausen, *L'Humanisme Agissant de K.M.,* 105.
7. Quoted in Fontaine, "Le XXIIe Congrès du P.C.F."
8. Fraser & Natanson, *Leon Blum,* 165.
9. Otto Bauer, *Austrian Revolution,* 85f.
10. Ibid., 91. His account of how the masses were lulled comes to a climax on p. 94f.
11. D. W. Morgan, *Socialist Left & the German Rev.,* 106.
12. Ibid., 250.
13. Carsten, *Rev. in Central Europe,* 142, cites the section, and is used here; the citation is less complete in D. W. Morgan, 258.
14. D. W. Morgan, 258.
15. Ibid., 25.
16. Brailsford, *Across the Blockade,* 140f.
17. Ibid., 143.
18. For these negotiations, see D. W. Morgan, 323.
19. Graham, *New Gov. of Central Eur.,* 469.
20. Ibid., 427.
21. Dutt, *The Internationale,* 168; Anderson, *Masters of Russian Marxism,* 100.
22. Luxemburg, "The Russian Revolution," (Wolfe trans., see Bibliog.), 28, 35f, 39 [334, 339, 341]. Here and below, the page numbers in brackets refer to the German text in her *Gesammelte Werke,* Bd. 4.
23. Lenin, "Report . . . ," in his *Coll. Wks.,* 29:184f.
24. Lenin, *Proletarian Rev. and the Renegade K.,* ibid., 28:271–79.
25. Luxemburg, op. cit. (see note 22), 63–66 [356–58].
26. Ibid., 69, 68, 71 [359, 361f].
27. Ibid., 72 [362].
28. Ibid., 76f [362f].
29. Ibid., 77f [363].
30. Ibid., 78f [364].

31. Ibid., 79 [364].
32. Ibid., 80 [365].
33. Luxemburg, "Die Nationalversammlung," Nov. 20, 1918, in her *Gesammelte Werke* 4:409f.
34. Luxemburg, "Was will der Spartakusbund?" Dec. 14, 1918, *Gesammelte Werke* 4:447.
35. Luxemburg, "Ein gewagtes Spiel," Nov. 24, 1918, *Gesammelte Werke* 4:411, 413.
36. Luxemburg, "Parteitag der Unabhängigen SP," Nov. 29, 1918, *Gesammelte Werke* 4:427.
37. For this traditional rationale, cf. *KMTR* 3:31 et sqq.
38. The three passages by Barth cited here are from his memoirs, *Aus der Werkstatt der deut. Revol.*, 25–28.
39. D. W. Morgan, *Socialist Left and the Ger. Rev.*, 457.
40. Ibid., 457. 209.
41. Bernstein, "Was ist Sozialismus?" 163.
42. Ibid., 162.
43. Bernstein, *Der Soz. Einst und Jetzt*, 114; see also mention on 123. (This was the last chapter in the *first* edition.)
44. Cunow, "M. und die Dikt. d. Prol.," *Neue Zeit*, 155.
45. Ibid., 157.
46. This reference to the "neo-social-democratic movement" is explained in Draper, "The New Social-Democratic Reformism" (see Bibliog.).
47. Trotsky, *My Life*, 274.
48. Hillquit, *From Marx to Lenin*, 54f.
49. Ibid., 57–60.
50. Ibid., 57.
51. Kautsky, *The Dict. of the Prol.*, 42f, 44.
52. Ibid., 140 (trans. slightly revised).
53. Kautsky, *Soc. Dem. vs Com.*, 38–40.
54. Kautsky, *Die mater. Geschichtsauffassung*, 2:469.
55. Bernstein, *Der Soz. Einst und Jetzt*, 114.
56. Kautsky, *The Dict. of the Prol.*, 43.
57. Kautsky, *Soc. Dem. vs Com.*, 41.
58. Ibid., 41–45.
59. Ibid., 42.
60. Kautsky, *The Dict. of the Prol.*, 58, 141.
61. Kautsky, *Labour Revolution*, 85.
62. Kautsky, *The Dict. of the Prol.*, 140.
63. Ibid., 43 (trans. slightly revised).
64. The quote is from the end of Engels' 1886 preface to the English edition of *Capital*, Vol. 1.
65. Kautsky, *Labour Revolution*, 60 (trans. slightly revised).
66. See Chap. 4, Sec. 6, p. 000.
67. See, for ex., Lenin, *Proletarian Rev. and the Renegade K.*, in his *Coll. Wks.* 28:248f.
68. For ex., Lenin's first formulation: see Chap. 4, Sec. 1.

69. See Locus 9, in Chap. 1, Sec. 6, p. [41].
70. For Locus 12, see Chap. 1, Sec. 7, p. [45].
71. See Salvadori, *K. Kautsky and the Soc. Rev.*, 152–69.
72. Memoirs of V. D. Bonch-Bruyevich, quoted in ed. notes, Lenin's *Coll. Wks.* 28:512 n.90.
73. For the article, see Lenin, "The Defeat of One's Own Government," in *Coll. Wks.* 21:275 + ; for my discussion, Draper, "The Myth of Lenin's 'Revolutionary Defeatism' " (see Bibliog.).
74. See Chap. 4, Sec. 6.
75. See the discussion and references in Chap. 4, Sec. 1, note 11.
76. Lenin, *Proletarian Rev. and the Renegade K.*, in his Coll. Wks. 28:239, 240, 243, 245, 246, 251, 254.
77. Ibid., 250.
78. Ibid., 252.
79. Ibid., 235.
80. See Chap. 4, Sec. 5, esp. p. [135].
81. Lenin, *Proletarian Rev. and the Renegade K.*, in Coll. Wks. 28:254.
82. Ibid., 304.
83. Only an initial section was written up and published under the title "Economics and Politics in the Era of the Dictatorship of the Proletariat," in *Coll. Wks.* 30:107 + .
84. Lenin, "The Dictatorship of the Proletariat," ibid., 30:99.
85. Lenin, "Report . . . Eighth Congress . . . ," Mar. 19, 1919, in *Coll. Wks.* 29:183.
86. Lenin, "The Dict. of the Prol.," ibid., 30:103.
87. Lenin, *Proletarian Rev. and the Renegade K.*, ibid., 28:231.
88. Trotsky, *Terrorism and Communism*, 22.
89. Kamenev, *The Dict. of the Prol.*, 6.
90. Ibid., 11.
91. Bukharin, "Theory of the Dict. of the Prol.," 45, 48.
92. Radek, *Prol. Dict. and Terrorism*, 24f.
93. Trotsky, *Terrorism and Communism*, 69 + .
94. Ibid., 21.
95. Ibid., 36f.
96. Kamenev, *The Dict. of the Prol.*, 4–5.
97. Ibid., 14.
98. Trotsky, *Terrorism and Communism*, 107.
99. Ibid., 108.
100. Ibid., 109.
101. Ibid., 137 + .
102. Bukharin, "Theory of the Dict. of the Prol.," 47.

Special Note A. Charles Bonnier on 'Dictatorship of the Proletariat.'

1. Compère-Morel, *Grand Dictionnaire Socialiste,* 221f; Vérecque, 143.
2. The three installments appeared in *Le Socialiste* (Paris) on Dec. 27, 1896, and Jan. 3 and 10, 1897.

Special Note B. Supplement to Chapter 5.

1. Deutscher, *The Prophet Armed,* Chap. 14.
2. Ibid., 508.
3. Trotsky, *Stalinism and Bolshevism,* 22.
4. Ibid., 21.
5. Ibid., 22.
6. D'Agostino, *Marxism and the Russian Anarchists,* 163.
7. Serge, *Memoirs of a Revolutionary,* 120.
8. Avrich, *Russian Anarchists,* 201.
9. Ibid., 202.
10. D'Agostino, 164.
11. Bakunin, *Political Philosophy of . . .* (Maximov, ed.); the introduction by Rudolf Rocker has a brief memoir on Maximov, 25–27.
12. D'Agostino, 156, 164.
13. Ibid., 163.
14. Ibid., 168, 207.
15. Ibid., 248, 242–47.
16. See also excerpts from the Pauls' pamphlet *Communism,* as quoted in Postgate, *Out of the Past,* 72.
17. Paul, E. & C., *Creative Revolution,* 129, 130.
18. Ibid., 143–46, 38f.
19. Ibid., 116.
20. Ibid., 16, 22f, 33, 45, 73f.
21. Ibid., 180f, 187, 192f (on materialism); 20, 147.
22. Webb, S. & B., *Soviet Communism,* 1:441.
23. Webb, S. & B., *The Truth About Soviet Russia,* 77.
24. Ibid., 57.
25. Ibid., 58.
26. Ibid., 46.
27. Ibid., 50.
28. Shaw, *Rationalization of Russia,* 71.
29. For a summary of Shaw's piece, see my review in *New Politics,* Fall 1966, p. 94f.
30. Rappoport, "Marx et la Dict. de la Prol.," 167.
31. Ibid., 169.
32. Ibid., 170.
33. For the *Communist Manifesto,* see *MESW* 1:118. I discussed it in *KMTR* 3, Chap. 8, Sec. 2.
34. Miles, *Socialism's New Beginning,* 60, 62; see also 63.

35. Edinger, *German Exile Politics,* 99.
36. Ibid., 116f.
37. Ibid., all of Chap. 3; and see also Anderson, *Hammer or Anvil,* 164f.
38. Edinger, 91, 105, 115–117.
39. Quoted in Edinger, 108.
40. Buttinger, *In the Twilight of Socialism,* 155.
41. Ibid., 159, 162, 166; cf. also Edinger, 107.
42. See the review by Joseph Carter, *New International* (N.Y.), July 1934, p. 31.
43. This passage is based on personal memory; I do not have the documents on hand.

Bibliography
(Works Cited)

This list provides bibliographic data for titles referred to in the Reference Notes or in the text. It is not a general bibliography on the subject of this book.

Anderson, Evelyn. *Hammer or Anvil: The Story of the German Working Class Movement.* London: Gollancz, 1945.

Anderson, Thornton. *Masters of Russian Marxism.* New York: Appleton-Century-Crofts, 1963.

Avrich, Paul. *The Russian Anarchists.* (Studies of the Russian Institute, Columbia Univ.) Princeton Univ. Press, 1967; paperback ed. 1974.

Bakunin, Michael. *The Political Philosophy of Bakunin: Scientific Anarchism.* Compiled & ed. by G. P. Maximoff. Preface by B. F. Hoselitz. Introduction by Rudolf Rocker. Glencoe, Ill.: Free Press, 1953.

Baron, Samuel H. *Plekhanov, the Father of Russian Marxism.* Stanford Univ. Press, 1963.

Barth, Emil. *Aus der Werkstatt der deutschen Revolution.* Berlin: A. Hoffmann's Verlag, n.d. [1919].

Bauer, Otto. *The Austrian Revolution.* Tr. by H. J. Stenning. London: Leonard Parsons, 1925. —Abridged version of his *Die Oesterreichische Revolution.*

Bernstein, Eduard. *Evolutionary Socialism: A Criticism and Affirmation.* Tr. by E. C. Harvey. (Socialist Lib., 7) New York: B. W. Huebsch, 1909. — Trans. (lacking two chapters) of his *Die Voraussetzungen des Sozialismus und die Aufgaben der Sozialdemokratie.*

————. *Der Sozialismus einst und jetzt. Streitfragen des Sozialismus in Vergangenheit und Gegenwart.* Zweite, vermehrte Auflage. (Internationale Bibliothek, 82) Berlin: Dietz Nachf., 1923.—The first ed., 1922, lacked Chap. 10–11.

————"Was ist Sozialismus?" in his *Ein revisionistisches Sozialismusbild.* Hrsg. & eingeleitet von Helmut Hirsch. (Internationale Bibliothek, 95) 2. Auflage. Berlin: Dietz Nachf., 1976.

Brailsford, H. N. *Across the Blockade. A Record of Travels in Enemy Europe*. New York: Harcourt, Brace & Howe, 1919.

Bukharin, Nikolai. "The Theory of the Dictatorship of the Proletariat." In his *The Politics and Economics of the Transition Period*. Ed. with intro by K. J. Tarbuck. Tr. by Oliver Field. London: Routledge & Kegan Paul, 1979. — First pub. in a collection of articles *Oktiabr'skii pererorot i diktatura proletariata*, Moscow, 1919.

Buttinger, Joseph. *In the Twilight of Socialism. A History of the Revolutionary Socialists of Austria*. New York: Praeger, 1953.

Carsten, F. L. *Revolution in Central Europe, 1918–1919*. Univ. of Calif. Press, 1972.

Compère-Morel, Adéodat. *Grand Dictionnaire Socialiste*. Paris: 1909.

Cunow, Heinrich. "Marx und die Diktatur des Proletariats." In *Die Neue Zeit*, Jg. 38 (1919/20), Bd. 2, p. 152+.

D'Agostino, Anthony. *Marxism and the Russian Anarchists*. San Francisco: Germinal Press, 1977.

Dan, Theodore. *The Origins of Bolshevism*. Ed. & tr. by Joel Carmichael. Preface by Leonard Schapiro. New York: Harper & Row, 1964; paperback, New York: Schocken, 1970.

————"Les Socialistes Russes et la Dictature du Prolétariat." In: T. Dan & J. Martov. *La Dictature du Prolétariat*. (Pages Socialistes, 9) Paris: Eds. de la Liberté, 1947.—The lecture by Dan was originally pub. as a pamphlet, with the same title, Paris: Bibliothèque de la Bataille Socialiste, 1934.

Deutscher, Isaac. *The Prophet Armed. Trotsky: 1879–1921*. New York, London: Oxford Univ. Press, 1954.

Draper, Hal. "Bang!" [Review of Shaw's book.] In: *New Politics* (New York), Fall 1966, p. 94.

————Karl Marx's Theory of Revolution. Vol. 1: *State and Bureaucracy*, 1977. Vol. 2: *The Politics of Social Classes*, 1978. Vol. 3: *The 'Dictatorship of the Proletariat,'* 1986. New York: Monthly Review Press, 1977+.

————"Marx and the Dictatorship of the Proletariat." In: *Etudes de Marxologie* (Paris), No. 6, Sept. 1962.—Condensed version in *New Politics* (New York), Summer 1962, p. 91+.

————"The Myth of Lenin's 'Revolutionary Defeatism.'". In: *New International* (New York), Sept./Oct., Nov./Dec. and Jan./Feb. 1953–54 (3 installments).

————"The New Social-Democratic Reformism." In: *New Politics* (New York), winter 1963, p. 100+.

Dutt, R. Palme. *The Internationale*. London: L&W, 1964.

Edinger, Lewis J. *German Exile Politics: The Social-Democratic Executive Committee in the Nazi Era*. Univ. of Calif. Press, 1956.

Encyclopaedia of the Social Sciences. Ed. by E. R. A. Seligman. New York: Macmillan, 1930–35; reissued 1937. 15v.

Fontaine, André. "Le XXIIe Congrès du P.C.F." In: *Le Monde*, Feb. 4, 1976.

Fraser, Geoffrey, and Thadee Natanson. *Leon Blum, Man and Statesman*. (Left Book Club ed.) London: Gollancz, 1937.

Frölich, Paul. "Einleitung." See: Luxemburg, Rosa. *Gegen den Reformismus*.

Getzler, Israel. *Martov. A Political Biography* . . . Cambridge Univ. Press, 1967.

Graham, Malbone W., Jr. *New Governments of Central Europe.* New York: Henry Holt, 1924.

Hardy, Deborah. *Petr Tkachev, the Critic as Jacobin.* Univ. of Washington Press, 1977.

Hillquit, Morris. *From Marx to Lenin.* New York: Hanford Press, 1921.

Hook, Sidney. *Marx and the Marxists; the Ambiguous Legacy.* Princeton: Van Nostrand (Anvil Original), 1955.

Jaurès, Jean. *Etudes Socialistes.* 5. éd. Paris: Société d'Eds. Litt. et Artistiques, 1902.

Kamenev, L. B. *The Dictatorship of the Proletariat.* By L. Kameneff. London: Communist Party of G.B., n.d.—Text is dated June 1920.

Kautsky, Karl. *Bernstein und das sozialdemokratische Programm. Eine Antikritik.* Stuttgart: Dietz Nachf., 1899.

————*Communism in Central Europe in the Time of the Reformation.* Tr. by J. L. & E. G. Mulliken. London: T. Fisher Unwin, 1897.

————*The Dictatorship of the Proletariat.* Intro by John H. Kautsky. [Tr. by H. J. Stenning.] (Ann Arbor Paperbacks) Univ. of Michigan Press, 1964.—Tr. of his *Die Diktatur des Proletariats.* Vienna, 1918. This poor translation was first published by the I.L.P.: 2d ed., Manchester: National Labour Press, n.d. [1920].

————*The Labour Revolution.* Tr. by H. J. Stenning. London: Allen & Unwin, 1925.—This English ed. omits first section of the German original, dealing with program revision.

————*Die materialistische Geschichtsauffassung.* Zweiter Band: *Der Staat und die Entwicklung der Menschheit.* Berlin: Dietz Nachf., 1927.

—*The Road to Power.* Authorized tr. by A. M. Simons. Chicago: Progressive Woman Pub. Co., c1909—Tr. of his *Weg zur Macht* (q.v.).

—*Social Democracy versus Communism.* Ed. & tr. by David Shub & Joseph Shaplen, with intro by Sidney Hook. New York: Rand School Press, 1946.

—*Die Vorläufer des neueren Sozialismus.* Erster Band, erster Theil: Von Plato bis zu den Wiedertäufern. (Series: *Die Geschichte des Sozialismus in Einzeldarstellungen,* von E. Bernstein et al.) Stuttgart: Dietz, 1895.—An edition much revised in format was published as: *Vorläufer des neueren Sozialismus.* Zweite, durchgesehene Auflage. Erster Band: *Kommunistische Bewegungen im Mittelalter.* Stuttgart: Dietz Nachf., 1909.

————*Der Weg zur Macht.* Hrsg. und eingeleitet von Georg Fülberth. Frankfurt: Eur. Verlagsanstalt, 1972.—First pub 1909.

Keep, J. L. H. *The Rise of Social Democracy in Russia.* Oxford: Clarendon Press, 1963.

Landauer, Carl. *European Socialism.* Univ. of Calif. Press, 1959. 2v.

Laurat, Lucien. *Marxism and Democracy.* Tr. by Edw. Fitzgerald. London: Gollancz, 1940.

Lenin, V. I. *Collected Works.* Moscow: FLPH (Vol. 1–19) and Progress Pub., 1960–70. 45v.—The following writings are cited from this set. The numbers after the title give volume and initial page. Dating abbreviations: (W) = written; (P) = first published. Writings originally published as pamphlets or books are italicized.

Can the Bolsheviks Retain State Power? 26:87. (W) Sept.–Oct. 1917.

A Caricature of Marxism and Imperialist Economism. 23:28. (W) Aug.– Oct. 1916.

Concluding Speech on the Report of the Council of People's Commissars, Jan. 25 (Third All-Russ. Congress of Soviets, Jan. 1918). 26:473.

A Contribution to the History of the Question of the Dictatorship. 31:340. (W) Oct. 20, 1920.

The Defeat of One's Own Government in the Imperialist War. 21:275. (P) July 26, 1915.

The Dictatorship of the Proletariat. 30:93. (W) Sep.–Oct. 1919.

The "Disarmament" Slogan. 23:94. (W) Oct. 1916.

Draft and Explanation of a Program for the S.D. Party. 2:93. (W) 1895– 96.

Draft Program of Our Party. 4:227. (W) End of 1899.

Draft Program of the R.S.D.L.P. 6:27. (W) Jan.–Feb. 1902.

Draft Resolution for the C.C., R.S.D.L.P.(B.) Concerning the Expulsion from the Party of S. A. Lozovsky. 42:49. (W) Jan. 1918.

Draft Resolution for the Third Congress of the R.S.D.L.P. 8:195. (W) Feb. 1905.

Draft Theses to the Resolution on the Soviets. (Seventh All-Russia Conference of the Party, May 7–12, 1917.) 24:255. (W) May 1917.

The Dual Power. 24:38. (P) Apr. 9, 1917.

Economics and Politics in the Era of the Dictatorship of the Proletariat. 30:107. (P) Nov. 7,1919.

An Epidemic of Credulity. 25:65. (P) June 21, 1917.

Fear of the Collapse of the Old and the Fight for the New. 26:400. (W) Jan. 6–9, 1918.

How the "Spark" Was Nearly Extinguished. 4:333. (W) Sept. 1900.

The Immediate Tasks of the Soviet Government. 27:235. (W) Mar.–Apr. 1918.

Karl Marx. 21:43. (W) July–Nov. 1914. (P) 1915 in *Granat Encyclopaedia*.

Left-Wing Childishness and the Petty-Bourgeois Mentality. 27:323. (P) May 9–11, 1918.

Material for Working Out the R.S.D.L.P. Program, (2) and (4). 41:39, 46. (W) Jan.–Feb. 1902.

New Tasks and New Forces. 8:211. (P) Mar. 8, 1905.

Notes on Plekhanov's Second Draft Program. 6:37. (W) Feb.–Mar. 1902.

On the Slogan for a United States of Europe. 21:339. (P) Aug. 23, 1915.

One Step Forward, Two Steps Back. 7:203. (W) Feb.–May 1904.

Outline of Plekhanov's First Draft Program . . . 41:39. (W) By Jan. 21, 1902.

Ozvobozhdeniye-ists and New Iskrists, Monarchists and Girondists. 8:221. (P) Mar. 8, 1905.

Plekhanov on Terror. 42:47. (P) Jan. 4, 1918.

Preface to the Russian Translation of W. Liebknecht's Pamphlet. 11:401. (W) Dec. 1906.

The Proletarian Revolution and the Renegade Kautsky. 28:271. (W) Oct.–Nov. 1918.

The Proletariat and Its Ally in the Russian Revolution. 11:365. (W)(Dec. 1906.

Reply to P. Kievsky. 23:22. (W) Aug.–Sept. 1916.

Report at the Second All-Russ. Trade Union Congress, Jan. 20, 1919. 28:412.

Report of the Council of People's Commissars, Jan. 26, 1918 (Extraord. All-Russ. Railwaymen's Congress, Jan.–Feb. 1918). 26:484

Report on Foreign Policy delivered at a joint meeting of the All-Russ. C.E.C. and the Moscow Soviet, May 14, 1918. 27:365.

Report on the Current Situation, May 7 (Seventh All-Russ. Conference of the Party, May 7–12, 1917) 24:228.

Report on the Immediate Tasks of the Soviet Government. (Session of the All-Russ. C.E.C.) Apr. 29, 1918. 27:279.

Report on the Party Program. Mar. 19 (Eighth Congress of the R.C.P.-B., Mar. 1919). 29:165.

Report on the Question of the Participations of the Social-Democrats in a Provisional Revolutionary Government. May 1 (The Third Congress of the R.S.D.L.P., Apr.–May 1905). 8:382.

Review; Karl Kautsky, *Bernstein und das soz.-dem. Programm.* 4:193. (W) End of 1899.

Revision of the Party Program. 26:149. (W) Oct. 1917.

Six Theses on the Immediate Tasks of the Soviet Government. 27:314. (W) Apr.–May 1918.

Some Sources of the Present Ideological Discord. 16:87. (P) Dec. 1909.

Speech at a Ceremonial Meeting of the All-Russia Central and Moscow T.U. Councils. 28:132. (P) Nov. 6, 1918.

Speech at a Rally and Concert for the All-Russia Extraordinary Commission Staff, Nov. 7, 1918. 28:169. (P) Nov. 9, 1918.

Speech at the Second All-Russia Congress of Internationalist Teachers, Jan. 18, 1919. 28:407.

The State and Revolution. 25:381. (W) Aug.–Sept. 1917; 2d ed., Dec. 1918. (P) 1918; 2d ed., 1919

Theses on the Constituent Assembly. 26:379. (W) Dec. 1917.

Two Tactics of Social-Democracy in the Democratic Revolution. 9:15. (W) June–July 1905.

The Victory of the Cadets and the Tasks of the Workers' Party. 10:199. (W) Apr. 1906.

What Is to Be Done? 5:346. (W) Autumn 1901 to Feb. 1902.

Lidtke, Vernon L. *The Outlawed Party. Social Democracy in Germany, 1878–1890.* Princeton Univ. Press, 1966.

Liebknecht, Karl. "Die neue Methode." In: *Die Neue Zeit,* Jg. 20, Bd. 2, Nr. 23, 1901/02.

Liebknecht, Wilhelm. *On the Political Position of Social-Democracy . . . No*

Compromises, No Election Deals. The Spider and the Fly. Moscow: FLPH, n. d. [after 1958].—The first two of these three speeches were made 1869 and 1899 resp.

Longuet, Charles. "Marx et la Commune." In: *Le Mouvement Socialiste,* Jan. 15, 1901, Vol. 5, No. 50.—This was his preface to the forthcoming French tr. of Marx's *Civil War in France.*

Luxemburg, Rosa. *Gegen den Reformismus.* Bd. 3 of her *Gesammelte Werke,* hrsg. von Clara Zetkin & A. Warski. Eingeleitet and bearb. von Paul Frölich. Berlin: Vereinigung Int. Verl.-Anst. GMBH, 1925.—This ed. is cited only for Frölich's introduction.

————*Gesammelte Werke.* Hrsg.: IML beim ZK der SED. Berlin: Dietz, 1970–75. 5v. in 6 (Bd. 1 in two volumes).

————*Politische Schriften.* Hrsg. und eingel. von O. I. Flechtheim. Frankfurt: Eur. Verlagsanstalt, 1966–68. 3v.

————*The Russian Revolution* and *Leninism or Marxism?* New intro by B. D. Wolfe. (Ann Arbor Paperbacks) Univ. of Michigan Press, 1961.

Martov, Julius. "Marx and the Dictatorship of the Proletariat." In his *The State and the Socialist Revolution* (q. v.).—First published 1918.

————*The State and the Socialist Revolution.* Tr. by Integer. New York: International Review, 1938.

Marx, Karl, and Friedrich Engels. *Selected Works in Three Volumes.* Moscow: Progress Pub., 1969–70.—Abbreviated: *MESW.*

————*Werke.* Institut für Marxismus-Leninismus beim ZK der SED. Berlin: Dietz, 1956–68. 39v plus supplements.—Abbreviated: *MEW*

Miles [pseud.] *Socialism's New Beginning: A Manifesto from Underground Germany.* Tr. from the German *Neu Beginnen.* Prefaces by H. N. Brailsford and Norman Thomas. New York: L.I.D., 1934.

Morgan, David W. *The Socialist Left and the German Revolution. A History of the German Independent Social Democratic Party, 1917–1922.* Cornell Univ. Press, 1975.

Nenni, Pietro. *Ten Years of Tyranny in Italy.* Tr. by Anne Steele. London: Allen & Unwin, 1932.—Originally pub. in French, 1930.

Paul, Eden & Cedar. *Creative Revolution: A Study of Communist Ergatocracy.* New York: Thomas Seltzer, 1920.

Plekhanov, Georgi V. *Selected Philosophical Works.* Moscow: Progress Pub., 1960–81. 5v. (Vol. 1, 3d ed., 1977.)—Tr. by various hands.

Postgate, Raymond W. *Out of the Past: Some Revolutionary Sketches.* Boston: Houghton Mifflin, 1923.

Radek, Karl. *Proletarian Dictatorship and Terrorism.* Tr. by P. Lavin. Detroit: Marxian Educ. Society, n.d. [1921].

Radkey, Oliver H. *The Agrarian Foes of Bolshevism.* Columbia Univ. Press, 1958.

————*The Sickle Under the Hammer: The Russian Socialist Revolutionaries in the Early Months of Soviet Rule.* Columbia Univ. Press, 1963.

Rappoport, Charles. "Marx et la Dictature du Prolétariat." In: *Revue Communiste,* 1920. p. 162–72.

Salvadori, Massimo. *Karl Kautsky and the Socialist Revolution 1880–1938.* Tr. by Jon Rothschild. London: NLB, 1979.

Schapiro, Leonard. *The Communist Party of the Soviet Union*. New York: Random House, 1959.

Serge, Victor. *Memoirs of a Revolutionary 1901–1941*. Tr. & ed. by Peter Sedgwick. London: Oxford Univ. Press, 1967 (paperback); first pub. 1963.

Shaw, Bernard. *The Rationalization of Russia*. Ed. with an intro by Harry M. Geduld. Indiana Univ. Press, 1964.

Sombart, Werner. *Socialism and the Social Movement*. Tr. from the 6th German ed. by M. Epstein. London: Dent; New York: Dutton, 1909.—First ed. pub. 1896.

Somerhausen, Luc. *L'Humanisme Agissant de Karl Marx*. Préface de Bracke. Paris: Richard-Masse, 1946.

Sturzo, Luigi. *Italy and Fascismo*. Preface by Gilbert Murray. New York: Harcourt, Brace, 1926.

Trotsky, Leon. *My Life: An Attempt at an Autobiography*. New York: Scribner's, 1931.

————*Our Revolution: Essays on Working-Class and International Revolution, 1904–1917*. Collected & tr. by M. J. Olgin. New York: Holt, 1918.

————*Stalin. An Appraisal of the Man and His Influence*. Ed. & tr. by Charles Malamuth. New York: Harper, 1941.

————*Stalinism and Bolshevism: Concerning the Historical and Theoretical Roots of the Fourth International*. New York: Pioneer Pub., 1937.

————*Terrorism and Communism. A Reply to Karl Kautsky*. Foreword by M. Shachtman. (Ann Arbor Paperbacks) Univ. of Michigan Press, 1964. Also published in English under other titles, including *The Defense of Terrorism*.

Venturi, Franco. *Roots of Revolution. A History of the Populist and Socialist Movements in Nineteenth Century Russia*. With an intro by Isaiah Berlin. Tr. by Francis Haskell. New York: Grosset & Dunlap, 1966.—English tr. first pub. 1960.

Vérecque, Charles. *Dictionnaire du Socialisme*. Paris: Giard & Brière, 1911.

Webb, Sidney and Beatrice. *Soviet Communism: A New Civilisation?* New York: Scribner's, 1937, c1936.—New ed., 1941, with a new intro, removed the question mark from the title.

————*The Truth About Soviet Russia*. With an essay on the Webbs by Bernard Shaw. New York, London: Longmans, Green, 1942.

Wolfe, Bertram. *Three Who Made a Revolution: A Biographical History*. Boston: Beacon Press, 1955; c1948.

Index

This Index does not cover the Reference Notes or the Bibliography. There is no listing for geographical terms and subject headings which occur so abundantly that a long list of page numbers would be of little use. Topics under these subjects should be sought under headings of a narrower scope. Types of 'dictator(ship)' are listed under that word; e.g., 'military dictator(ship),' etc. Titles of books or other writings are indexed only for substantive references, not if merely quoted or mentioned; the same applies to names of periodicals. If the title itself is not indexed, see the author's name.

Reference to a page includes footnotes on that page. Reference to a footnote only is indicated by *n;* thus 94n = footnote on page 94. An *f* means "plus page following"; thus 114f = pages 114–115. "Passim" is shown by three suspension points between page numbers; thus 81 . . . 85 = pages 81–85 passim, that is, the subject is implicit or explicit throughout these pages.